CHURCH IN HISTORY SERIES

The Church in a Changing World

EVENTS AND TRENDS FROM 250 to 600

BY
MARIANKA S. FOUSEK

CONCORDIA PUBLISHING HOUSE
ST. LOUIS   LONDON

ACKNOWLEDGEMENTS

The author thanks these publishers for permitting the use of their copyright works:

The Catholic University of America Press: *Fathers of the Church*, Vol. 5, tr. V. J. Bourke, © 1953; Vol. 9, tr. M. M. Wagner, © 1950.

The Clarendon Press: *Didascalia Apostolorum*, tr. and ed. R. H. Connolly, © 1929.

The Macmillan Company and Geoffrey Bles, Inc.: Athanasius, *On the Incarnation of the Word of God*, s. nn., 1946.

Oxford University Press: *Documents of the Christian Church*, Henry Bettenson, © 1947; "Sing, My Tongue, the Glorious Battle," tr. P. Dearmer (1867–1936), alt. by permission.

Paulist/Newman Press: *Ancient Christian Writers*, Vols. 25, 31, 33, ed. Joh. Quasten and W. J. Burghardt; *Sources of Christian Theology*, Vols. 1 and 2, ed. P. F. Palmer; *Patrology*, Vol. 2, ed. Joh. Quasten.

Philosophical Library: *Letters of St. Athanasius Concerning the Holy Spirit*, ed. C. R. B. Shapland, 1951.

The Society for Promoting Christian Knowledge: *A New Eusebius*, J. Stevenson, © 1965.

The Westminster Press: *Christology of the Later Fathers, LCC*, Vol. III, ed. Edward R. Hardy and Cyril C. Richardson, 1954; *Early Latin Theology, LCC*, Vol. V, tr. and ed. S. L. Greenslade, 1956; *Western Asceticism*, Vol. XII, ed. Owen Chadwick, 1958.

Concordia Publishing House, St. Louis, Missouri
Concordia Publishing House Ltd., London, E. C. 1
Copyright © 1971 Concordia Publishing House
Library of Congress Catalog Card No. 77-139331
ISBN 0-570-06272-1
MANUFACTURED IN THE UNITED STATES OF AMERICA

To all who want the church
to be a living challenge
to their world

CONTENTS

Maps/6

Chronological Overview/8

Introduction/10

1. Church and Society in a Changing World/12

2. Worship, Devotion, and Art/28

3. Faith and Teaching/55

4. Structure, Leadership, and Service/82

5. Monasticism, the New Leaven/99

6. St. Augustine, the Great Teacher of the West/117

Appendix: Readings from Primary Sources/128

Suggestions for Further Reading/172

Index/174

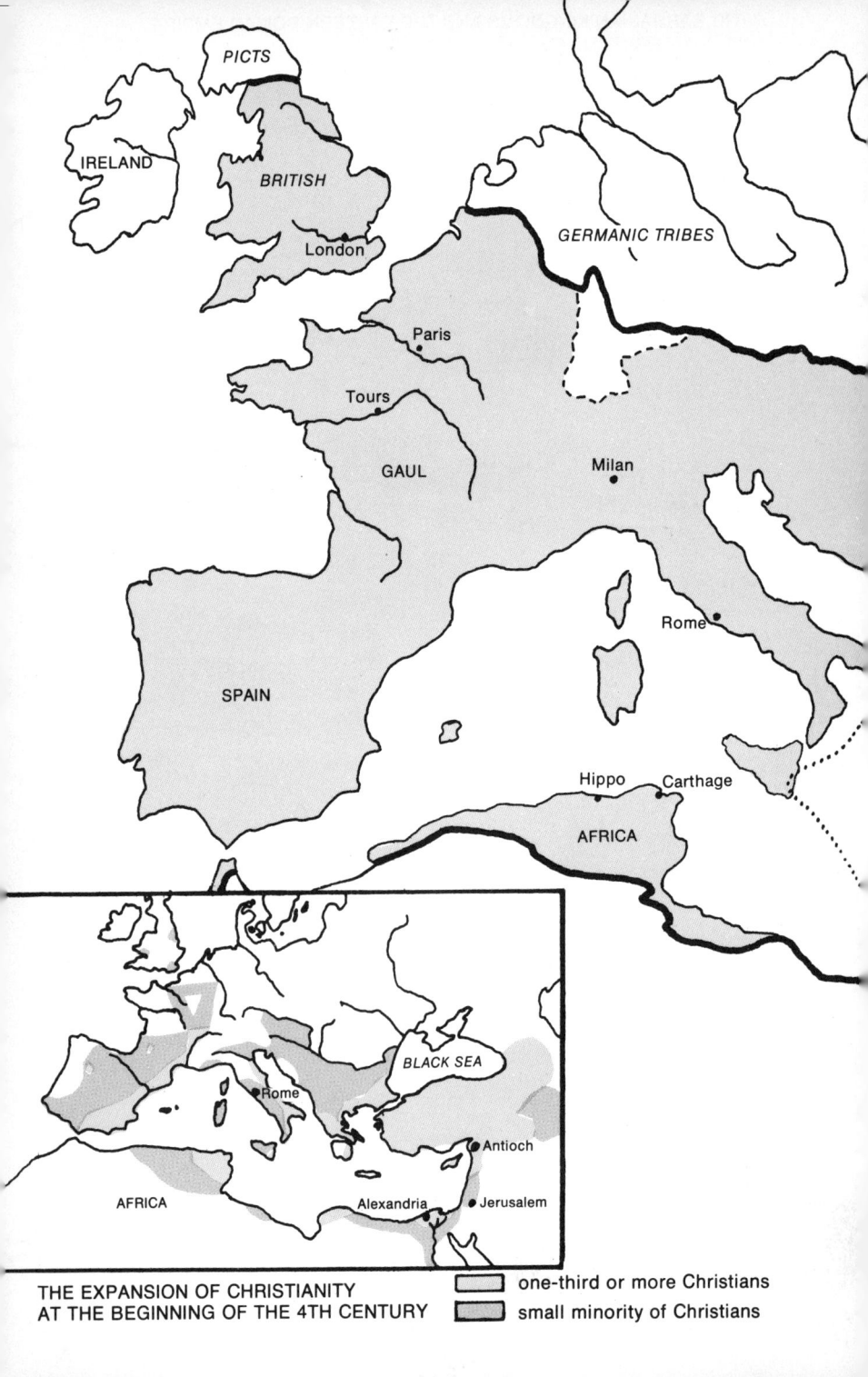

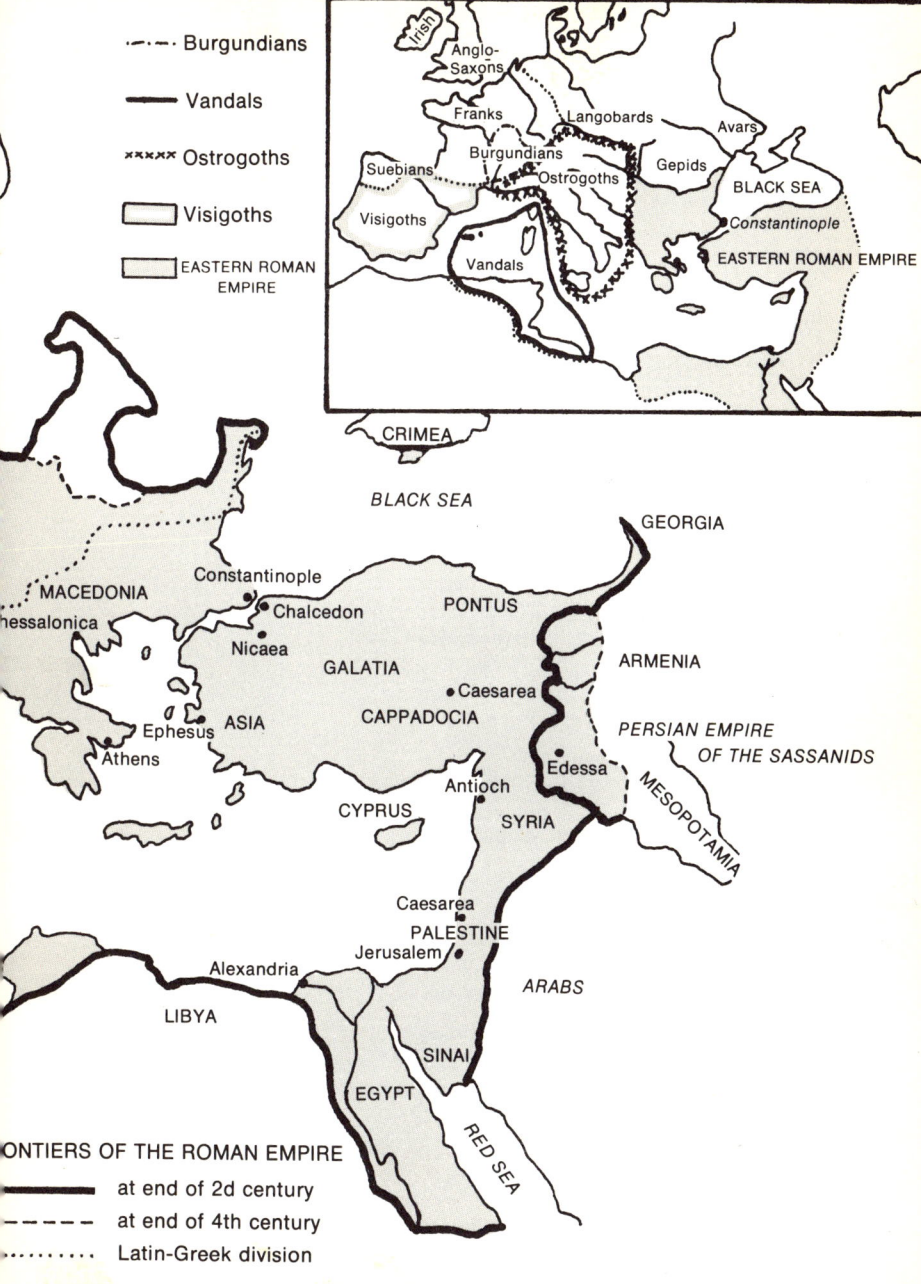

Center map based on Jean Daniellou and Henri Marrou, *Nouvelle Histoire d' Eglise*, I. *(The First 600 Years)*, Paris, 1963.

Corner maps based on *Atlas of the Classical World*, ed. A. A. M. Van der Heyden and H. H. Sullard, Nelson's, 1959.

CHRONOLOGICAL OVERVIEW

WORLD EVENTS	CHURCH EVENTS	LITERATURE
	Mid-3rd Century	
Rise of Manicheanism and Neoplatonism	Cyprian, bishop of Carthage	Cyprian's writings
	First empirewide persecutions	
Decius, emperor 249-251	Schisms over the lapsed	
	"Great Peace of the Church" (Long toleration)	
	Anthony, 1st Christian hermit	
	Church condemns Monarchian doctrines	
	King of Armenia accepts Christianity	
	4th Century, 1st Half	
Diocletian, emperor 284-305	Diocletian persecution	Athanasius' writings
	Donatist schism	
	Pachomius founds 1st monastery	"Sayings of the Desert Fathers" circulate
Constantine, sole emperor 324-337	Final freedom for Christians	
	Arian controversy erupts	Eusebius collects primary sources for his "Ecclesiastical History"
	Council of Nicaea, 325	
Constantinople founded	King of Georgia, a Christian	
	Wulfilla (Arian), missionary to the Goths	

	4th Century, 2nd Half	
Emperor Julian Apostate (360-363) attempts to revive paganism	Three great Cappadocian bishops Eastern monasticism reformed Ambrose, bishop of Milan Conversion of Augustine	Golden Age of Christian Literature Writings of Cappadocians Writings and preaching of Ambrose
Emperor Theodosius (379-395) makes "Catholic" Church the church of the empire	Jerome at Bethlehem Beginnings of Christological controversies John Chrysostom	Jerome's Vulgate, letters Chrysostom's sermons
	End of 4th Through 5th Centuries	
Onslaughts by Huns, Vandals, Visigoths	Controversies with Manicheans, Donatists, Pelagians, pagans climax Christological controversies St. Patrick's mission	Augustine's writings
	Leo the Great, pope Council of Chalcedon, 451 Christological schisms	"Tome of Leo" Definition of Chalcedon
	6th Century	
Emperor Justinian (527-565) attempts but fails to wrest the West from the barbarians Justinian Code Lombards invade Italy	Baptism of Clovis, king of Franks St. Columbia's mission and "Rule" Height of Byzantine art St. Columbanus' mission to Gaul	"Rules" of Celtic monasticism St. Benedict's "Rule"
	Turn of the 7th Century	
	Gregory the Great, pope (died 604) His mission to England	Gregory's writings

INTRODUCTION

Our own era is marked by revolutions and dramatic changes among the nations in the areas of culture, social mores, worldviews, philosophy, technology, and our whole way of life. The church is caught up in the midst of the swirl.

When we consider the period of this volume: the years between A. D. 250 and 600, we see that the society and church of those days underwent similar earthshaking changes. That era of tremendous upheavals necessitated adjustments as great as ours. Around A. D. 250 it saw the first systematic persecution of Christians by the Roman Empire, which had begun to feel threatened by the spiritual challenge of the growing Christian movement. In the early 4th century, almost overnight, came a period of imperial favor for the church and a wide acceptance of Christianity by society. Within less than a century came the collapse of the Roman world in the West under the impact of barbarian invasions. The church then entered an entirely new and unfamiliar world, which it undertook to win for its faith. The years around A. D. 600 saw chaos-driven Western Christendom obtain the history-making leadership of Gregory the Great, who is considered the last great "Father" of the ancient church and a founder of the medieval papacy.

How did the church fare in these periods of persecution or seductive favor? Did its devotion, thought, and

INTRODUCTION

leadership grow, or did these become stale and irrelevant with the advance of time? How much real influence did Christianity exercise on society? How did the church adjust to the disappearance of the familiar Roman world and to the chaos and new societies that succeeded the Roman order? Did this era of changes produce any significant developments that endure to this day?

Our aim is to probe the life and thought of the church in the changing world of this era.

1.

CHURCH AND SOCIETY IN A CHANGING WORLD

ORDEAL BY FIRE

The first period of the great changes started in the mid-3rd century and lasted for almost 75 years. It brought fierce, intermittent, empirewide persecutions of Christians. It was for the Christian community, grown large and soft by the security it had enjoyed for most of the preceding half century, a trial by fire.

The first great persecution began in 250, when the new emperor Decius launched a new policy requiring all citizens to sacrifice to the pagan gods and to have a certified statement (a *libellus*) of their compliance with the edict. The Roman Empire had suffered serious setbacks in the preceding years. It was generally believed that the ancient gods were revenging themselves on the empire for its lax policy toward the Christians, who refused to worship the gods and who influenced others to neglect their civic duty toward them as the divine patrons of the empire. Many Christians could not bring themselves to face the fierce penalties and so either performed the required ritual or at least secured the *libellus* from friendly or bribed officials. The leaders of the church naturally considered such acts a repudiation of the baptismal vow, by which the baptized had foresworn all pagan gods and bound themselves only to the one God. The fallen, or *lapsed*, Christians were barred from the church's Communion until they showed sufficient penitence and received reconciliation from the Christian community, the household of God.

The number of the "lapsed" was alarming. As many as 80 percent of some congregations' members were classed among the public "penitents," once the rugged but brief first wave of the great persecutions was over. Other waves followed. The last universal and greatest persecution took place under Emperor Diocletian in 303-4. He ordered all Christian churches to be destroyed, Christian sacred books and vessels confiscated, and all Christian clergy imprisoned. Finally, all citizens were required to sacrifice to the gods or face death. The persecutions tested the church's mettle, restored it to its unique calling within society, and renewed its spiritual vigor. The church was being prepared for a role of leadership in Roman society, a role which fell to it with the final victory of Constantine when he became the sole ruler of the Roman Empire in the autumn of 324.

THE SURPRISING VICTORY

The definitive end of the persecutions and Christianity's sudden rise to imperial favor and prominence in Roman life came as a surprise to the church. From its beginning the church had been a small and often suspect minority.

Constantine was a military leader. He turned to the Christians' God for aid in battle, and when he won he became devoted to the Christian church. There is the famous story of his vision of the cross and the words, "By this sign conquer,"[1] inscribed on the midday sun. Another story tells of a dream in which Constantine was told to put the XP (pronounced Ki-Ro)[2] monogram on the shields of his soldiers to secure victory.

We may have doubts about the depth of Constantine's understanding of the Christian faith and of his conversion, but the emperor was after all a military man, for whom victory in battle was crucial. Although he never became a man of peace, his legislation as emperor testifies to his Christianity.

He forbade the branding of prisoners on the face, "because man is made in the image of God." He directed all prisons to let the inmates out into the open air each day, so that a day may not pass without their having seen the salutary sun. Constantine also assigned a large portion of the government's revenues to the support of the philanthropic work maintained by the church (a work which was not being undertaken by any other organization or agency; the church was a pioneer in the works of mercy). He built magnificent large churches, exempted the clergy from taxes, and made Christian clergymen paid civil servants of the empire.

His support of the church was a mixed blessing. It radically altered the status of the Christian in society and the life and makeup of the Christian community. It became easy to become a Christian and advantageous to enter the clergy. The meaning and cost of discipleship became all too often obscured, and many people entered the ranks and offices of the church without conviction.

THE MARRIAGE OF FAITH AND CULTURE

Constantine must have hoped that the empire-wide Christian church would become the cement which would unite the badly-cracking empire and give it a sense of common purpose and dedication. The Roman Empire had become too huge and heterogenous to have such a unity of itself. It contained many annexed and conquered provinces, and its population and army included more and more immigrants from the nomadic Gothic (that is, Germanic) tribes who were pressing in on the empire from several directions. To stem the inflow of immigrants, the imperial officials sometimes refused them permission to settle on Roman land, an action which evoked successive Gothic invasions of the empire. To guard the security of its frontiers, the state needed inner unity in its population and army. There was nothing corresponding to the American school system, with its Americanizing effect on immigrants, to unite the empire. The cult of the emperor, designed to develop a common loyalty in the empire, had failed in its purpose.

The Christian church was the only institution that might perhaps weld the people into one. Thus the emperors initiated the marriage of church and society. We use the image of marriage purposefully, for marriage means union and not identity, and it involves give-and-take, adjustments, crises, and storms.

Society was not immediately Christianized, of course, nor was Christianity the state religion under Constantine. Christians were then only a substantial minority. It was not until the end of the 4th century, under Emperor Theodosius, that the church became the state church and that laws were issued against public pagan worship. Pagans still continued to hold high positions in the empire until the mid-6th century, when Emperor Justinian outlawed paganism. Jews were protected by imperial law, even if they were not always free from molestation. Yet Christianity was obviously the imperially favored religion, and a harmony and cooperation between church and state was the envisioned ideal. More and more people poured into the church. The church had an opportunity to influence the society; it became wide open to the existing culture, with its riches and its problems.

The 4th century was the "Golden Age" of Christian antiquity. The accumulated learning, arts, and skills of the Greco-Roman and Near Eastern civilizations were now absorbed by the church without fear of heathen contamination. The pagan culture ceased to appear dangerous. Most of the best minds embraced the faith which had been considered vulgar and low-class by the educated classes only a short while before. The result was a flourishing of Christian literature and theology, of skillful preaching, and of the arts connected with Christian worship and devotion.

The Christianization of a whole society and its

culture was a difficult and long-term task. Many of the existing cultural and social forms and customs had to be adapted, and they transformed only very gradually. The church engaged in a vigorous teaching activity, not only in preaching but also in the preparation of candidates for their baptism. But the former rigorous screening of these catechumens fell into disuse. The church now rejoiced at having the opportunity to reach the multitude.

There was a parallel growth of Christian ranks outside the Roman circles. However, while Christianity within the empire spread by and large simply by "contagion," it was often brought by specific individuals to the nations outside the Roman confines. There were, however, no "missionary societies." Since, in contrast to the population of the Roman Empire, most of these peoples had a strong sense of their corporate unity, whole tribes and kingdoms accepted Christian baptism. The majority of the Gothic peoples (in and outside the empire), several Arab tribes, the kingdoms of Armenia, Georgia, and Ethiopia, as well as the Franks, the Irish, the Scots, and finally the English had become or were to become Christian between the end of the 3rd and the end of the 6th centuries. (Christianity also penetrated from Christianized Syria into Mesopotamia and Persia even though it was not favored by the Sassanite rulers, the great rivals of the Roman emperors.) The traditions and folklore of the baptized peoples were also "baptized" in the process. A most striking example of this is the introduction of Christmas into the church's calendar. It was typical of the fusion of formerly pagan customs with Christian celebrations. The early Christians considered the celebration of Jesus' birthday unnecessary or even inappropriate. No one knew when Jesus was born. It was not customary to celebrate people's birthdays. The emperors' birthdays may be feted, but Jesus was not an emperor, Origen (3rd century) curtly said.

In the West December 25 and in the East January 6 were popular holidays in honor of the birth (return) of the sun. Eastertime roughly coincided with spring fertility rites.

When the church wanted to win the masses in the 4th century, it was good psychology to transform the pagan feast days into Christian festivities. The Christian acceptance of the ancient pagan lore of the new converts explains the many otherwise illogical customs associated with the Christian holy days, such as Easter eggs and bunnies.

Not only *harmless* pagan traditions found their way into the church. Some pagan ideas were irreconcilable with Christian teaching and values and gave the church a hard struggle or actually a new face.

The 4th to the 6th centuries were marked by violent theological debates and by conflicts between bishops and emperor. The great theological question of the time dealt with the relationship of the transcendent God to the world and to human existence. Much of Greek and Oriental philosophical thought made an absolute separation between the infinite and the finite; between the spiritual and the earthly. If there was such an infinite chasm between these spheres, how could God create the world or have any relationship with it? How could men know God? How could the infinite God enter history or human existence and redeem it? Who, then, was Jesus Christ and what did He accomplish? These questions affected the heart of the Christian faith; they were fought over bitterly, with a Greek philosophical thoroughness that sometimes seems pointless to the practical Western mind.

Although these controversies often appear to have been only wrangles over words, ultimate questions were at stake. They also often involved open conflict between the church's leaders and government officials who wanted to achieve peace and unity in church and empire by means of compromise. The emperor considered himself responsible for his entire realm, and in his mind theological matters were not separable from it. Recalcitrant bishops were usually deposed and exiled, but the emperors were only temporarily successful in imposing their will on the church's creeds. At other times emperor and bishop faced each other over questions of imperial policy and practice in the social realm. The church was by no means separate from the state and, although the church did not wish a separation, the truly great bishops, whether in the East or West, were no puppets of the imperial court. The 4th to the 6th centuries provide a rather fascinating history of church-state relations.

Among the most dangerous results of the marriage of church and society in the 4th century was the transmission of the easygoing ways and values of society into the church. Power, ease, and comfort changed the church from an elite minority into a comfortable, all-inclusive church which could no longer be distinguished from the rest of society. Discipline and self-sacrifice were not its marks. Its life had ceased to be an inspiration and challenge to men.

It is against this background that we must understand the rise and attraction of Christian monasticism. The 4th century ascetic movement arose as a protest against the loss of the heroic nature of the church. The early hermits and monks wanted to obey Jesus' demand to "sell all" and "follow" Him on His hard and lonely way. They wished to bear His cross and follow in the footsteps of the martyrs who bore witness to their Master by their rejection and agony. Wonderful as it was that society no longer wanted to suppress the Christian faith and that it even wished to embrace it, the change in social status robbed the church of its heroic character and blunted the sharp edge of the Gospel for the multitude and the highborn who were now entering it. The men and women who were enthralled by the monastic ideal in this period knew the cost of Christian discipleship and wanted to pay it. Since the age of the martyrs was in the past, the hermits and monks became the new heroes of Christendom. They were a constant challenge to the superficially Christian society.

How great was the actual Christian influence on Roman society and government? Although it is difficult to assess such a complex matter, the influence seems disappointing. It was impossible really to convert a whole ancient culture and a totalitarian system of government within a few generations. By the turn of the 4th century the imperial government had indeed become totalitarian out of the fear of collapse before the onslaught of continued invasions and mutinies. Nevertheless, the church did have an important role and considerable influence within the given limits.

The most striking example of the Christian influence was the introduction of *the 7-day week* into Roman society and from there eventually into other parts of the world. The system of dividing time into weeks, with one day as a holiday, was completely unknown outside Jewish and Christian circles. When Constantine and his successors made Sunday an official day of rest, it was a tremendous boon to the working man, and it provided a new rhythm of life in society. Under Christian influence concubinage for a married man was forbidden, adultery and rape became more severely punished, divorce was made less easy, and infanticide became illegal (but not the abandonment of infants; a Roman father had the right to dispose of his newborn children). The immensely popular, bloody spectacle of gladiatorial contests in the circus shows were not discontinued until well over 100 years after Constantine's conversion. The lot of slaves and prisoners became somewhat humanized during the first 100 years of the rule of Christian emperors. In the sale of slaves it was forbidden to separate the members of a family (a regular practice in modern Christian America until about 100 years ago), and the freeing of slaves was made easier. Jailers were forbidden to starve prisoners and were commanded to bring them to the baths once a week. But the torture of prisoners suspected of any antisocial activities was a regular feature of the system. It should be noted that even prior to the Christian impact, reforms in the status of slaves had been effected as a result of Stoic philosophical influence on emperors. It is sometimes difficult to distinguish between Stoic and Christian influence in the framing of more humanitarian laws.

Landed aristocrats were quite free to do as they pleased with the farmers on their estates. While the slaves there received better status, the peasants became bound to the soil and were almost slaves in their standing. The institution of serfdom was beginning to emerge, and neither the government nor the church was particularly effective in checking the oppression by the wealthy.

On the whole, the church was not an effective agent of social reform. Originally a small voluntary brotherhood awaiting the end of this world with its injustices, it was not prepared to reform an empire. The church was not a group of plotting social revolutionaries. It probably would have taken a revolution to shake up the structures of the entrenched society. It took the barbarians to do that. Except in time of war, barbarian customs and laws were less savage than those of the late Roman Empire, corrupted as it was by wealth, power, and fear. Still, the bishops were able to be a saving or chastening influence in many individual instances. Bishops could intercede with the authorities on behalf of accused or threatened individuals or cities, and in the ancient world the intercession of respected persons counted heavily. So Bishop Flavian averted a major disaster from the city of Antioch, whose population expected fearful reprisals for their rioting and smashing of the emperor's statues when an increase in the already oppressive taxation had been announced. Bishop Ambrose of Milan for a while persuaded Emperor Theodosius not to wreak bloody revenge on the population of Thessalonica for its riots against the imperial troops stationed there. When the emperor in hot temper changed his mind and had 7,000 unsuspecting Thessalonians massacred in the circus to which they had been invited by subterfuge, Ambrose announced he would not give the emperor Communion until he had submitted himself to public penance—and the emperor complied.

Perhaps what the church lacked was more men like Ambrose, though unfortunately he did not use his skill and power always for the benefit of justice. A better balance of power in the empire was what the welfare of the society needed. If all power had not been concentrated in the hands of the emperor and of the extremely rich, Christian social teaching could have made the church more effective. Or, would a greater emphasis on a Biblical understanding of social justice in the Christian training of the emperors' and aristocrats' children have done the job? Would the parents have kept such disconcerting tutors?

In the sphere of philanthropy the church did make a genuinely pioneering impact on its society. The church was able to introduce the principle of compassion for the weak (pity for the weak was scorned by pagan philosophy) and a sense of the dignity of the less fortunate members of society. In the Christian understanding, the rich bestowing gifts on the underprivileged were not considered as their generous benefactors but as following simple justice (this, by the way, was a part of the Christian's Jewish heritage) and as doing themselves actually a favor, for the poor were considered specially close to Christ. Their intercessions for their donors were respected as having special weight with God. Thus the commonly accepted practice and notion of intercession was reversed; here the poor were the powerful intercessors and therefore benefactors of the disadvantaged rich. The wealthy may have their money, but the poor have their prayers. This tipped the balance.

In addition to the church's care for needy individuals and its encouraging generosity and interest on the part of the wealthy Christians in this work, the church (richly endowed by imperial and private monies and wills, the latter especially bequeathing large tracts of fertile land to the church) pioneered in the development of institutions and professional staff for the care of the sick, especially the lepers, the insane, the homeless, the poverty-stricken, and the travelers. These works of the church provide the foundation of all modern institutions of this nature. The church's influence of instilling a compassionate attitude in the minds of the people toward the less fortunate may have been the most revolutionary principle introduced into civilization, even if its full effect has been felt only in modern times and often in secular guise.

The church exhorted slaveowners and other men with legal powers over people to be humane. In the case of slavery, the church encouraged the freeing of slaves and accepted slaves as important officeholders in the church. Slaves were certainly not segregated from freemen in church. Nevertheless, the church did not seriously try to reform the structure of society and its laws. Instead of trying to change the system, earnest Christians simply tended to shrink from being in a position which would involve them in unchristian actions, at least during the earlier part of the era under our survey. During the 3rd and 4th centuries it was not at all clear to Christians whether they could be soldiers or magistrates (which involved judicial responsibilities) with good conscience. Although Christians were usually allowed to remain or become soldiers during peacetime, they were not allowed to shed blood or torture anyone even when under orders. The same held true for Christians in the position of judges. Given the harsh laws of the era and the common practice of judicial torture, it is easy to see why Christians would initially avoid the office. If a Christian as a magistrate or soldier became responsible for the torture or death of a man, he was to abstain from Communion and undergo the prolonged penance customary for grave sins. In the 5th and 6th centuries, when society became almost wholly Christianized on the surface, it became inevitable and acceptable that Christians should assume all the burdens of law-and-order enforcement, including the use of violence on behalf of the safety of the empire, as long as the war could be considered morally justified and was conducted without barbarism.

It is hard for us to see why Christians in influential positions did not try to change the laws more radically, though of course the ability to reform the rules of war has eluded us to this day. The resignation of the church to the brutalities of the Roman legal system, with all its inequalities and with slavery and torture as a part of it, seems to have come from an unquestioning identification of the "world" with the society they knew. They had no illusions about the nature of the "fallen" world, and since they knew no social system other than their own, they assumed that such aberrations as legal inequalities, torture, and capital punishment were as much an inevitable, even if a deeply deplorable, part of the fallen world as were social inequalities, sickness, and death. Their realism about the world made them accept the use of external, often brutal, force and restraint (laws) as a means of curbing violence and chaos in the world.

Now that the Christians assumed responsibility for their world (which the *early* Christians, a small minority which felt quite apart from it, really did not and did not need to do), they became its reluctant guardians and defenders against external attacks. They assumed one could do little to alter the basically oppressive nature and the social inequalities of the secular community. This was why the clergy merely tried to ameliorate the situation by attempting to shape a more humane conscience among men. They confined themselves to this instead of attacking the basic structure or at least some of the laws of the socially-stratified and totalitarian Roman Empire in its later period. It is of course an unanswerable question whether the Christians could have succeeded, had they attempted it. For one thing, the church's marriage with society tied its hands and also made it accustomed to its ways. For another, the empire was anything but a democracy.

A NEW SOCIETY REPLACES THE OLD

The world in which the church found security by Constantine's victory did not last long. Early in the 5th century Roman power in the western part of the empire collapsed under the assault of invading Germanic tribes. In 410 the Visigoths under Alaric sacked Rome. In 429 the Vandals crossed the Strait of Gibraltar and flooded Roman North Africa, only to return to sack Rome in 455. The emperor, however, continued to reside in Constantinople, the "new Rome" built by Constantine on the strategic site of old Byzantium on the Strait of Bosporus as the imperial residence and headquarters of the empire. The empire was able to hold its own in the East, but the West was for all practical purposes lost to the barbarians. Germanic chieftains and kings, together with able bishops, replaced the imperial rule and administration there.

It fell to the lot of Christian bishops to restore order out of the chaos and to maintain a measure of safety and well-being for their people. It was often the bishops who led the defense of their towns and negotiated the peace with the barbarians. It was the bishops and monks who carried on the educational and feeding activities formerly provided by the government (the latter as the Roman counterpart to our food-stamp program). They preserved and passed on whatever could be salvaged of Roman order and civilization, worked for a peaceful coexistence between the old population and the new settlers, and exerted themselves for the extension of the orthodox Christian faith in the new kingdoms. The greatest leadership in these respects was provided by some of the bishops of Rome.

Most of the barbarians (so-called because of the unintelligibility of their speech to the Greco-Romans, to whom their words sounded just as so many "bar, bars") did not wish to destroy the Roman Christian civilization for which they held the highest admiration. They hoped to reap its benefits. They were driven into the Roman Empire by their flight from the savage Huns, who had displaced them from the East. Thus the efforts to extend to them the Roman Christian culture and faith were not in vain, and in time a synthesis of the two worlds — Latin Christian and barbarian — emerged. It was the making of the new Christian Europe.

EAST-WEST CLEAVAGE

The barbarian take-over in the West naturally created a deep wedge between the eastern and western parts of the empire and thus between Eastern and Western Christendom. The Latin-speaking West always had a somewhat different mentality and type of civilization than the Greek-speaking East. Broadly speaking, the West (the Romans proper) was more practical-minded than the more philosophically and mystically inclined Greek East. The West, except for a few great metropolitan centers like Rome and Milan in Italy and Carthage in North Africa, was also always more rural in character than the urban civilization of the Greco-Roman East. Culture was more refined and more advanced in the East; the West had imported Eastern culture and imitated it. The Roman higher classes were educated by Greek masters and learned the Greek language. The great intellectual centers — the universities and libraries — were in the East, where the arts and commerce also flourished. The East provided the church with its greatest theological teachers.

The barbarian seizure of the West stopped the interchange and communication between the East and the West. The Westerners no longer learned Greek; they were happy if they could maintain (or learn) even a simplified Latin in their lands. The imperially maintained city schools disappeared and the cities themselves almost did, too. The barbarians were a rural folk, and the Roman cities were devastated. It was only the old Roman landowning families and the bishops and monasteries who preserved (or copied) the remainders of the Roman libraries and learning. The cultural impoverishment of the West and its separation from the Greek East created an estrangement between the churches of the East and West. The lack of contacts between them and the development of different conditions and traditions in the East and West led to misunderstandings, suspicions, and schisms between Eastern and Western Christendom. The real division between the Eastern Orthodox and Western Christians stems from this period, resulting in two different Christian histories.

Both church and state and their mutual relationship developed along different lines in western Europe and in the Orthodox Byzantine Empire, as the eastern part of the empire came to be called (from Byzantium, the old name of Constantinople). The patriarch-bishop of Constantinople could never develop a very strong or independent position for his office. He was curtailed by the proximity of a powerful emperor and was hemmed in by the other great patriarchates of the East, especially by Antioch and Alexandria. The tragic history of St. John Chrysostom, who dared to criticize the conduct of the empress and of unworthy bishops and who was ruined by them and by the intrigues of the jealous partriarch of Alexandria, is a glaring example. Thus Byzantine Christendom never developed anything parallel to the power and authority of the pope in the West.

The patriarch-bishop of the West, the pope of Rome, had no real rival counterparts in the West. His bishopric inherited both the ancient glory of the church in Rome, with its claim to a link with the apostle Peter, and much of the prestige and responsibilities of imperial Rome after the emperor had left for the East. With the emperor far away, the Roman patriarch could usually act independently of the emperor. Most of the smaller bishops and other clergy, as well as the population, looked to him for leadership and help. The various barbarian chieftains and kings recognized the prestigious nature of his venerable office. Moreover, the papal office was occupied by several remarkable men, culminating in Gregory the Great at the end of our period. The Western Church and society for several centuries found their natural leaders in the Roman popes.

The old Roman population had a hard time accepting the collapse of its world. The end of "eternal Rome" seemed an impossibility and the greatest imaginable calamity. It was fortunate that the church was able to divorce itself from the old order and perceive a providential design in the history of the times. St. Augustine, who died during the Vandal siege of his African city Hippo in 430, bequeathed to Western Christians in his *City of God* an interpretation of history, which helped them and succeeding generations to see the transitoriness and corruption of every social order and yet the role each has in divine providence. He pointed out that the church, the agent of the "City of God," must operate within every city of man and yet distinguish itself from it, functioning as its light. Thus the Latin church accepted the new order of things and

CHURCH AND SOCIETY IN A CHANGING WORLD

set out to win the new societies and shape them. Its success was not a little due to the prestige of Christian Rome among the barbarians and to the influence of the popes, bishops, monks, and prominent Christian wives who made the orthodox Christian faith attractive to the heretical (Arian) or heathen barbarians. Missionary monks, such as Sts. Patrick, Columba, and Augustine of Canterbury and their disciples converted Ireland, Scotland, and England in the 5th and 6th centuries.

The close of our age was marked by a clarification and definition of the church's credal standards. The canon of the Bible had largely been settled by then, and the orthodox creed regarding the person of Christ had been defined. The church developed a great reverence for the "Fathers," its great teachers and the writers of the past, and for the councils of Christian antiquity. The age of creative theological work in the West gave way to the age of preserving and of handing on the great tradition to succeeding generations. This was the beginning of the early Middle Ages, when the Eastern world and church guarded, developed, and eventually passed on to others their Byzantine-Greek culture and orthodoxy, while the Latin church began to be shaped by and to shape the new nations which replaced the old world of the western Roman Empire.

Notes

1. The Latin *In hoc signo vinces* is usually rendered in the abbreviated form of *Hoc signo*, or as *Nika* in Greek, and is used as a Christian symbol.
2. In Greek the letters *X* (Chi) and *P* (Rho), form the beginning of the name "Christ." The letters, one superimposed on the other, became yet another Christian symbol.

2.

WORSHIP, DEVOTION, AND ART

The central act of the assembled Christian community was the Eucharist, or Holy Communion, celebrated by the ancient church every Sunday and on all festival days. The primary form and spirit of this service was that of thanksgiving (the literal meaning of the Greek word *eucharistia*) and of a joyous celebration. It was a great thanksgiving for the creative and redemptive work of God in Christ, a celebration of Christ's life-giving presence among His people, a communion of the entire church on earth with the church in heaven, and a pledge of the great reunion of all the faithful at the eternal banquet of God.

The highly symbolic partaking of the (leavened) bread and wine was seen as a festal meal where the Christian community received its continuous nurture for the new and eternal life which the Holy Spirit had implanted in its members at Baptism. The bread stood for the basic staple of life, for Christ is "the Bread of Life" (John 6:35) and gives daily sustenance to the soul.[1] The wine represented the quenching of thirst and the festive and inebriating nature of the occasion. Christ is the "true Drink," as St. Ambrose explained. "As often as you drink it, you receive the remission of sins and are inebriated in spirit."[2] The Eucharistic bread and wine were seen as "figures" of that which they became by the power of consecration—by the Eucharistic prayer or by the Eucharistic words of Christ recited by the priest—namely, the body and blood of Christ.[3] Christ was seen as giving Himself and His life to His people, uniting the believers with Himself and with one another. "The union is complete and eliminates all separation." "He unites Himself with their bodies so that mankind too, by its union with what is immortal, may share in incorruptibility."[4] "He who has eaten this Body, will receive remission of sins and 'shall not die forever' (John 6:50-58)."[5] "In the figure of bread is given to you His Body and in the figure of wine His Blood; that by partaking of the Body and Blood of Christ you might be of the same body and blood with Him. For thus we come to bear Christ in us, because His Body and Blood are diffused through our members; thus it is that, according to the blessed Peter, 'we become partakers of the Divine nature.' (2 Peter 1:4)"[6]

During the first three centuries all Christians in good standing partook of the Eucharistic meal every Sunday, and it was brought each time to all the sick members so that none of the faithful might miss such a great privilege. As the masses began to pour into the church after Constantine's conversion, fewer people came to partake of the Eucharist for fear of unworthy communion. Many stayed at the service merely as onlookers. Many church leaders, fearing superficial conversions, now stressed the awesome character of the Communion.

Christians thought of the Eucharistic service as representing the entire saving work of Christ, with the thought that the thankful recalling of it in prayer made it a present reality before God and themselves, and as an offering of themselves and of their world to God. Thus they spoke of it as the sacrifice of the New Covenant: an action whereby the sacrifice of Christ was made present and an offering of thanksgiving on their part.

Though there was a common structure to all Eucharistic services, different geographic regions had their own editions of the service, with significant variations in detail. At first there was place for free prayer on the part of the officiants, following the overall established tradition as to the main contents and style of the prayer, but by the latter part of the 4th century, with the liturgy more formalized, the prayers became set. The liturgical year, with its feasts and seasons, provided for the needed variety and at the same time for stability in the service. The liturgy was chanted, a custom of ancient origin. The chanting of the words made them more mysterious as well as more audible.

The leader of the community's worship was the bishop or the presbyter (priest) as his delegate. Other presbyters and deacons present served as assistants. The officiants faced the people during the liturgy. Originally the clergy wore no special vestments, and liturgical colors were unknown. Early Christians even scoffed at the idea that their clergy should be distinguished by something external such as clothes. Their ministers wore the same clothing as the Roman population: a long white, close-fitting, shirtlike tunic, later called alb (from *alba vestis*, "white garment" in Latin), girded around the waist. For public occasions they wore also a large white woolen circular overgarment, like an Indian poncho, with a hole for the head, flowing freely over the body; this came to be nicknamed *casubla* (chasuble in English), or a "little house" in Latin, because it housed the entire body. It was only when Roman clothing gave way to the Germanic fashions that the clergy started to look different from the lay people. The church, having become conservative, kept the old clothing for its officials, refusing to follow the winds of fashion. In this way the church unconsciously developed a uniform for its clergy, a special clothing which has come to be invested with deep symbolic significance. The alb and the chasuble are still the essential Eucharistic vestments (the chasuble mostly somewhat altered in color and cut) in Eastern Christendom, in Roman Catholicism, Scandinavian Lutheranism, and High Anglicanism.

Ancient Christians prayed standing or kneeling prostrate. The most common form and the only one thought fitting for Sundays and feast days was standing, a posture of free men and of exaltation. This was the general custom of all ancient worshipers. Their eyes, arms, and hands were raised toward heaven and their thoughts to God. They were not introverts probing their inner selves in prayer. The sign of the cross was used frequently from early times. It was a tangible way of realigning oneself with Christ, who on the cross triumphed over the powers of evil, and of recalling one's baptismal seal.

With the advent of Christian emperors, Christian assemblies became huge. Large and magnificent churches were built to house them. Christ was now thought of as the heavenly Emperor, the Ruler of all *(Pantokrator* in Greek), and His assembly on earth as reflecting the glory of His heavenly court. A splendid liturgical ceremonial developed, especially in the East, patterned after the formalities of the imperial court. In imitation of the imperial ceremonies, incense found its way into the liturgy. Originally it had been a token of the divine honors paid to gods and deified kings. Large choirs, often antiphonal double choirs answering one another in music, enhanced the beauty of the service. A sense of awe and mystery came to predominate both in the liturgy and in the building.

The music used in Christian worship was apparently the common music of the time, related to the type of music we associate with the Near East and with the Gregorian chant. The Psalms were the most ancient and beloved hymnbook of the church, but new hymns were composed, too, especially in the East. The most famous Latin hymn writers of our period were bishops Ambrose of Milan of the 4th century and Venantius Fortunatus of the 6th century. Hymns and canticles from this era are among the great ornaments of liturgies and hymnals to this day. Gregory the Great, who introduced some reforms into the singing at Rome, was eventually credited with the creation of the Roman musical system, the so-called "Gregorian chant," although he was not its inventor.

THE LITURGY

Although the following observations do not hold for every region and for every period, we shall try to give a general idea of the progression of the Eucharistic service as it emerged in the East and in the West when the lines had become set. The service was termed the "divine liturgy" *(leitourgia* meant "public work" in ancient Greek) in the East and gradually came to be called "mass" in the West, from the late Latin *missa,* first used for the "*dismissal*" or blessing at the end of the service and then, by extension, for the service itself.

The service did not open with a confession of sins. Such a practice became customary in the West in the later Middle Ages, but at this time confession did not form part of the public service. The liturgy was divided into two main parts. The first part, the service of the Word or "the liturgy of the catechumens," centered on the Word of God. It was so called because it was open to the catechumens, but they had to leave prior to the second part, the liturgy of Thanksgiving, that is, the Eucharistic liturgy proper. For this reason the first part, corresponding to a typical Protestant service today, is also called the Ante-Communion.

The liturgy opened with a procession, accompanied by chanting. The book of readings from the Gospels was brought to the altar during the procession. At the beginning there was also a solemn litany, or responsive prayer, led by the deacon. The simple response on the part of the people, *Kyrie eleison* (Greek for "Lord, have mercy!"), forms the first part of a mass set to music today. It is the so-called ninefold *Kyrie.* Such a litany is typical for the prayers of the people in the entire Eastern liturgy, reappearing in it several times. The form of this prayer, in particular the address *Kyrie eleison,* was taken over from cries addressed by the populace to the emperor as he passed in a triumphant procession through the streets. It was not a cry for pity, as it is often misrepresented to be, but an acclaim of the ruler and a petition for generosity in the distribution of gifts to the people. In church the cry was addressed to Christ, the heavenly King, and was followed by petitions for peace and well-being. It was not a penitential plea. A festive canticle could follow. In the East it was the "Holy and Mighty," and later in the West it was the *Gloria in Excelsis,* a hymn imported from the East. In the Latin rite, there next followed the short prayer called "collect," typical of the Western style of prayer. It is succinct, has one petition, and is rhythmic in style. Contrary to its traditional edition in English, the original Latin is extremely simple and clear, avoiding flowery language. A different collect was appointed for every Sunday and feast day of the year. It was meant to "collect" the silent prayers of the faithful which preceded it, and it was closed by an "Amen" on the part of the congregation. The "Amen" had become the people's endorsement of anything said or sung to them or for them. Then came the readings from the Scriptures, regional traditions determining what was read on the different Sundays and holy days. One lesson was always from the Old Testament. The lessons were followed by the homily, that is, the sermon. (The creed was borrowed from the baptismal service and was brought into the Eucharistic liturgy quite late, between the 5th and 8th centuries.)

The homily, normally based on a Biblical theme, was supposed to be an exposition of one of the Scripture readings. If the bishop and several presbyters were present, each could comment on the Scripture in turn. Many sermons, some excellent ones, are extant from this period. The 4th century St. John of Antioch and Constantinople, later nicknamed Chrysostom ("Of Golden Tongue"), was the most eloquent and perhaps the most moving of all the great preachers. He could sway his audience as he wished, and his congregation clapped in wild enthusiasm after his sermons. His sermons were distinguished by great simplicity and directness and by their deeply Biblical and pastoral nature. He spoke to his people.

After the sermon the catechumens and the public penitents were dismissed with a blessing and the second half of the service began. The faithful exchanged the "kiss of peace," as no one unreconciled to his brother was to bring an offering to God (Matt. 5:23 f.). Then the bread and wine, together with the other offerings (mostly in kind and not in money), were brought forward by the worshipers in a great offertory procession. The deacon took up the gifts after an initial dialog between the presiding minister and the congregation ("Lift up your hearts!" "We have them with the Lord") leading into the great Thanksgiving.[7] The presiding bishop or presbyter in charge then led the assembly in thanks for the creative and redemptive work of God in Jesus Christ. The action climaxed with the communal chanting of "Holy, holy, holy, Lord God of Sabbaoth," the recital of the Lord's words instituting the holy meal, and a petition for the life-giving action of the Holy Spirit (curiously missing from the Latin mass as it has come down to us). The whole church — all the living and the dead and especially the fellowship of saints — was remembered before God. The Eucharistic action was offered to Him as a spiritual offering. The prayers were ended by the "Our Father." The people came forward and, standing, received the bread and common chalice of wine into their hands from the bishop, presbyters, and deacon. With that the service was ended. People took home some of the unused consecrated bread as their daily link with the Sunday banquet.

BAPTISM

Baptism admitted a person, including children, to membership in the Christian church and its Holy Communion. Since most of the candidates in Roman society were adults coming from paganism, they were required to go through a lengthy period of instruction and spiritual preparation. This included exorcisms, the rituals for driving out the evil spirit. They were classified as "catechumens" (Greek for "those being taught") and stood in the back of the Christian assembly. Catechetical lectures and instructions to catechists from the 4th century are among the best expositions of Christian teaching and practice of the time.

Since Baptism was understood as a great watershed in people's lives, separating the old life from the new, it was taken with rather great seriousness. Baptism was seen as the washing away of all sin, the old self being buried with Christ, and the new self, bound to the risen Christ and filled with His Spirit, as taking the place of the old (Rom. 6:3-4).

> When you dip, you take on the likeness of death and burial, you receive the sacrament of the cross, because Christ hung on the cross and His body was transfixed with nails. You then are crucified with Him; you cling to Christ, you cling to the nails of our Lord Jesus Christ, lest the Devil be able to take you from Him. — At the selfsame moment you died and were born; and that water of salvation was at once your grave and your mother.[8]

The baptized person solemnly renounced Satan, the flesh (the old self), and the world with its pomp. This gave him privileges as well as obligations which he had not had before. Empowered by the gift of God's Spirit, he was expected to lead a new life. A breaking of his covenant was seen as a disaster, driving the Spirit away from him and barring him from communion with Christ and His family. It was only after a very heavy and long public penance, available only once in a lifetime to those who had been baptized, that sins considered deadly (killing the new life in a person) could be forgiven by the bishop, the heir of the apostles. This authority on the part of the bishop was based on these words of Christ: "If you forgive the sins of any, they are forgiven; if you retain the sins of any, they are retained" (John 20:23). Murder, adultery, and apostasy were held to be the most serious among the deadly sins.

Apostasy, or the falling away from the Christian faith, was the biggest problem during the empirewide persecutions in the latter half of the 3rd and the first part of the 4th century. Sexual offenses were the most common problem after Constantine's favorable policy toward Christianity, for the church now absorbed into its ranks masses of people unaccustomed to any discipline. The church in the 3rd and 4th centuries therefore warned people not to embrace Baptism too hastily, and many came to postpone it until after what were considered the dangerous years of adolescence. Some, like Constantine himself, who was not ready to pursue his politics according to Christian standards, waited even until old age or until shortly before death. The church naturally frowned on such practice. The fear to "soil one's Baptism" reflected paradoxically both the high regard in which Baptism was held and a growing unwillingness to accept the cost of being a disciple of Christ.

The rite of Baptism was normally received in the nude on the eve of Easter or at Pentecost, the latter especially in northern climates. It was composed of a series of symbolic anointings [9] and a bath or a pouring of water on the candidate standing in a body of water in the out-of-doors or in a specially built baptistry. Water was considered as both the symbol and the means of cleansing and as the source of life (John 3:5 ff.). Baptism brought a new birth. So we read in the catechetical instructions of Ambrose:

> Thus . . . in Baptism, since it is a likeness of death, undoubtedly, when you dip and rise again, it becomes a likeness of the resurrection. . . . You have read about the water, "Let the waters bring forth creatures having life, and creatures having life were born."[10]

The meaning and power of Baptism are set forth by John Chrysostom as including both the washing away of sins and the bestowal of new life:

> If the Bath takes away all sins, why is it not called the Bath of the remission of sins, or the Bath of cleansing, rather than the Bath of regeneration? The reason is that it does not simply remit our sins, nor does it simply cleanse us of our faults, but it does this just as if we were born anew. For it does create us anew and it fashions us again, not molding us from earth, but creating us from a different element, the nature of water.[11]

The final anointing of the head by the bishop and his laying on of hands on the head of the baptized person, believed to convey the gift of the Spirit (Acts 8:14-17), later developed in the West into the separate rite of confirmation. As a mark of the baptized one now belonging to Christ, the bishop "sealed" his forehead with the sign of the cross. All the neophytes then participated for the first time in Holy Communion.

When with the growth of rural parishes the bishop's flock became spread over too large an area, so that the bishop could not be present at all the baptisms, bishops in the West came to "confirm" the baptisms in the various parts of their overgrown parishes (dioceses) as opportunity presented itself. Confirmation, now separated from Baptism, was not a condition for admission to Holy Communion until after the time of Luther. The Eastern churches have no confirmation ceremony. The local priest receives oil (chrism) blessed by the bishop and anoints, or "chrismates," the baptized infants or converts in the name of the bishop.

The question concerning the baptizing of infants is not a simple one. It was certainly practiced in the ancient church, but how generally it is difficult to ascertain. As we see from an early 3rd-century baptismal liturgy, the baptism of very young children was considered normal in Rome, but Tertullian, a presbyter at Carthage at that time, advised to wait with baptism until a person had committed sins which call for such a washing. St. Cyprian, bishop of Carthage in Africa in the mid-3rd century, affirmed that children of church members ought to be baptized soon after birth because of the original sin in which they participate by virtue of being human. The Syrian liturgy, known as the "Apostolic Constitutions" from around A. D. 400, directs that children receive Communion right after the clergy. It would seem that as family unity was strong in the ancient world, the baptism of convert-parents, that is, their entrance into the church, usually made the baptism of their children seem natural. However, many realistic Christian parents wished their children to weather the years of youthful temptations before being baptized, so that they might not desecrate their baptism. In that case they entered their children as catechumens right after birth, a status which effected a connection with the church, offered some safety to the youngsters, and gave them a claim to receive Baptism in case of serious illness. The child was marked by the sign of the holy cross when he was entered as a catechumen. It was for such reasons that Monica entered her son Augustine as a catechumen while he was still in his cradle, purposely delaying his baptism. Augustine was baptized upon his conversion in his early thirties.

The postponement of baptism was not motivated by a desire to give the child the opportunity of a meaningful individual decision; such individualism was foreign to the family-minded ancients. Because of their deep faith in the life-giving qualities of the sacramental actions in Baptism and Communion, parents kept their children from early baptism only because of their fear of the grave consequences of breaking the baptismal vow. St. Augustine pressed for the universal baptism of infants because of his conviction that all men are born in original sin. Infant baptism soon became universal practice.

The church's mission to the so-called barbarian peoples, that is, to the nations outside the empire and to the tribes pushing into its confines, presented a unique challenge with regard to their instruction in the Christian faith and their baptism. The barbarian nations preserved a sense of corporate cohesiveness which the long-conquered and urbanized peoples of the Roman Empire had lost. Like the majority of Africans and Arabs today, the ancient Armenians, Georgians, and the various Germanic invaders felt themselves primarily members of their national or tribal groups. Their identity was not individualistic, nor did they feel themselves just members of their own families. Thus, to convert them individually or just in family groups would have meant breaking their natural ties. The only approach that could work without disrupting their way of life was to baptize the head of the tribe or kingdom and with him his entire people if they so wished.

Mass baptism was thus not necessarily a forced procedure but a natural one. After an elementary preaching of the Gospel to the chieftains and then to the multitudes, they were usually baptized together as a people. A more thorough catechizing and converting had to be postbaptismal and sometimes took generations. It can be asked whether the baptized barbarians were any less Christian in their beliefs and values than was the Roman population which pushed its way into the church with and after Constantine in a more individualized fashion. Once society became open to Christianity, the Christian community ceased to be an elite group. Wanting to reach as many as possible, the church became an inclusive body. This meant that the church had to come to terms with the world. In this it certainly did not go all the way, as we shall see from its penitential discipline and from the development of monasticism.

PENITENTIAL PRACTICES

The ancient church had a stringent discipline for its members. This was connected with its high view of Baptism and Communion and was derived from its understanding of its own nature as the new humanity, the new creation of God in Christ, the body of Christ imbued by His Spirit, the salt of the earth (Matt. 5:13), and the house of salvation. Thus the early church's members were trained and screened prior to their admission to membership—screened not regarding their former life but regarding the earnestness of their repentance. If they failed or "lapsed" in some gross way after baptism, they were excluded from the church's community. If they repented, they were subjected to a severe discipline which was called their second (that is, post-baptismal) repentance ("penance") or reconversion. The penitent confessed his sin to the bishop as the shepherd of the flock. The bishop prescribed a treatment which the church's tradition and his own discretion considered appropriate for the case. A part of the treatment was private, such as much prayer, fasting, gifts to the poor, abstinence from luxuries and pleasures, and a part was public. The public aspect of penance was exclusion from the church's Communion and self-humiliation before the brothers, whose forgiveness and prayers had to be sought. The penitents, together with the catechumens, stood in the back of the assembly, in the vestibule, or even behind the doors if their sins were extremely grave. However, no public confession of a secret sin was involved. At the end of the protracted penitential probation, the penitent was solemnly "reconciled" with the church by the bishop at a public service. The bishop prayed over him and laid his hands on his head, so that the Holy Spirit might descend on him again. Henceforth he was considered forgiven by God.[12]

The discipline was harsh, but it was considered medicinal rather than punitive: to heal the disease in the soul of the offender and in the body of the community, to prevent the spread of the infection,[13] to make token amends for the offense, and to have proof of the seriousness of his repentance. The community's dealing with the offender showed its solidarity and its caring as a community. Nobody lived or died to himself. The church and its leaders were responsible for the health of its members,[14] and the member was responsible to the community.

Connected with this was the fear of a sacrilegious participation in the Eucharist: a person communing unworthily is "guilty of profaning the body and blood of the Lord" and is condemned (1 Cor. 11:27). The church had to shield men from inviting judgment on themselves. The church, where men found the source and security of salvation, could not give people a false assurance of salvation, and this is why they believed offenders had to be excluded from the community pending their reconversion. Once they sincerely undertook the penance assigned to them, they could be sure of the mercy of God, *even prior* to their restoration to the communion of the church.

In addition to the official public penance for gross sins, there evolved the tradition of a voluntary private confession of the state of one's soul. It enabled the individual to go to freely-chosen spiritual guides to receive counsel, direction, and private discipline for his Christian life. The confessors could be not only bishops or ordinary presbyters but also spiritually-gifted laymen. Hermits and monks became especially sought out as wise confessors and counselors. The confessor might recommend to the penitent, for his voluntary observance, temporary abstention from the Eucharist as a form of penitential discipline. The penitent did not have to be formally forgiven by his confessor in order to be forgiven for his sins by God. Only the appropriateness and sufficiency of his private amends were under the confessor's moral authority.

Toward the latter part of the ancient era, when the church embraced all of society, public penance became almost extinct. Since the church had reacted with extreme sternness toward the lowering of standards within its ranks and had made the official penance unbearably long and hard, it became impossible for the bishops to insist on it. Private confession, however, remained and spread. Gradually it replaced public penance as the officially required church discipline for gross sins. Heinous sins, however, still called for solemn public penance. Eventually, but long after this period, private confession came to involve priestly absolution, a practice analogous to the reconciliation concluding the ancient public penance. As was pointed out before, there was no general confession and absolution in the church's Eucharistic liturgy.

With the influx of the masses into the church and the eclipse of its discipline, the church lost its character as the household of salvation. Now it became a "mixed church," which could give no assurance of salvation to its vast crowds. Salvation and eternal life now became not a present reality in the church as the tangible family of Christ, but merely an object of a pious hope for the individual beyond death and even beyond the purging fires which he might need before he was ready to enter into God's presence (compare this with the rising fear of the Holy Communion). Intercessory prayers and services for Christians who had died came to be seen as important means of delivering the faithful departed from the pains of the purgatorial (purging) process and of speeding them on to heaven.

OTHER SERVICES

Besides the services described so far, there were also early-morning preaching or instructional services in the churches on weekdays (though the growing custom of celebrating the Eucharist also on weekdays gradually replaced these) and several "hours" of psalm-centered "offices," that is, services, in the monastic communities. Some of the latter, like the early-morning matins and the evening vespers, found their way into the parishes.

A wedding was a family and civic transaction, not a church ceremony, though a bishop or his representative might be asked to bless the marriage.

The clergy apparently performed healing services over the ill, involving the anointing of the sick with oil, possibly a confession of sins, and prayers for forgiveness and healing (James 4:14-16). The Eucharist was brought to the bedside. Our information on the anointing of the sick in this period is too insufficient to establish what the exact practices might have been.

The service in memory of the dead was the Holy Communion, celebrated in consciousness of the communion between Christians on earth and the church beyond the sight of mortal men. There was a cosmic dimension to the church and its prayers.

THE DEVELOPMENT OF THE CHRISTIAN CALENDAR

The Christian calendar developed over many centuries. The first Christians kept the Jewish holy days, adding Sunday to them as a day on which to celebrate Jesus' resurrection. Sunday was not understood as a new Sabbath. The Sabbath was on Saturday and Jewish Christians continued to observe it as a day of rest and worship. Sunday was a workday until the time of Constantine, who made it a legal holiday. The early Christians met for their celebration of the Easter event every Saturday eve and then again on Sunday before sunrise. In the Near East, where the Christian church had its origin, days were reckoned from sunset to sunset, with the Sabbath beginning on Friday evening. Other holy days followed the same principle.

The first annual holy day which Christians developed was the annual Easter festival, considered the "Christian Passover," or the yearly celebration of the redemption of Israel from slavery and death. Jesus was seen as the new and perfect Passover Lamb, whose blood protects His people from destruction (Ex. 12:21-27 and 1 Cor. 5:7). In this celebration Jesus' death and resurrection formed an indivisible unity; there was for a long time no separate day for recalling Jesus' death. Redemption was grounded in Jesus' death and resurrection, and thus the two were seen as two sides of the one coin and were celebrated together during the Easter night.

Christians could not at first agree on when to celebrate the Christian "Pasch" (from *Pesach*, the Hebrew word for Passover), whether on the actual night of the Jewish Passover or on the Sunday of the first full moon after the vernal equinox, which is how the Passover date is determined each year.[15] After prolonged controversy the Sunday was selected as the universal day for the annual celebration of Easter as the "Christian Passover," because it was on a Sunday that Jesus rose from the dead.

The paschal (or Easter) celebration came to be

extended over a period of 50 days. The season—not just the 50th day—was called "Pentecost," from *pentekonta,* the Greek word for 50. It coincided, at least in principle, with the 50 days between the start of the Jewish Passover festivities and the Jewish Feast of Weeks, originally the early harvest ingathering which took place 7 weeks after the first Passover night. (Also the giving of the Law on Mount Sinai came to be celebrated during the Jewish Feast of Weeks.) The paschal season among Christians likewise had two high points: 1) Easter night, and 2) the day closing the festal season, that is, the 50th day after Easter. This was the day on which, according to Acts 2, the original disciples were given the Spirit. Both the Easter night and the 50th day—the day completing the Pentecost season—were favorite days for receiving catechumens into the church by baptism. There was also a two-day preparation for Easter, with the time marked by prayers and fasting—the germinal form of later Lent.

The paschal, or Pentecost, season celebrated redemption and the gift of the Spirit as present realities rather than as occurences in the dim past. This could be best seen in the ritual of baptism, by which the recipients were made participants in Jesus' death and resurrection, and in the bestowal of the Spirit. The celebration bridged the abyss of time and brought the past into the present moment, all of the redemptive acts coinciding in the "now" of the present. This was why the early Christians did not have separate days to recall all the different events which brought them their new life.

In addition to the paschal holy days, early Christians celebrated also the anniversaries of their local heroes' martyrdom. These deathdays were called the "birthdays" of saints entering the heavenly life. The faithful would gather at the tombs of the martyrs (often in catacombs) and joyfully celebrate the Eucharist together, in vivid awareness of their communion not only with Christ and one another but also with those of their heroic brethren who had gone ahead and were now at the throne of God. This practice was the origin of the saints' days.

In Jewish piety Tuesday and Thursday were fast days. The early Christians kept Wednesday and Friday as such fast days and called them "station days," or days of special religious vigilance. They were called station days in analogy to the station, or guard, which a soldier stands when he is on duty.

Just as the Easter celebration came to be extended forward, so on the other end it eventually also came to be anticipated by a lengthened period of preparation — from two days to two weeks, to 40 days, and to almost 70 days prior to Easter. Thus came about the Passion season, Lent, and Septuagesima (Latin for 70). The 40 days of Lent were developed before all else for the sake of catechumens and the public penitents. For the catechumens Lent formed the final weeks of instruction, scrutiny, and exorcism before their baptism on Easter night. This determined much of the character of Lent and helps to explain the choice of the traditional Gospel readings for most of the period. The accent of Lent was not on Jesus' forthcoming suffering but rather on His victorious power over the forces of darkness. The Gospel episodes read during this season concentrate on Jesus' triumph over the demonic in His wilderness temptation and on His healing of those possessed by evil spirits. They were meant to encourage the catechumens in their hope that the Lord, to whom they were turning, would be victorious also in *their* lives. Those who started their public penance at the beginning of Lent, as well as the members in good standing, were of course to receive similar encouragement from the lessons. The penitents who were to be re-admitted to the church's Communion received their reconciliation prior to Easter.

The final two weeks of Lent came to focus on Jesus' conflict with the authorities and on His suffering, or Passion (from *passio*, the Latin word for suffering). The entire pre-Easter period came to be considered a part of the paschal season.

With the emperors becoming Christian, a great

change came over the life of the church, affecting also the Christian holy days. With the freedom to celebrate Christian rites publicly and out-of-doors, there came the need to cope with the masses who were now attracted to Christian worship. Pilgrimages to the holy places of the Christian faith—sites connected with Jesus' life and with martyrs—became a possibility. Devotion, curiosity, and romantic feelings spurred thousands to become pilgrims. The Holy Land, especially Jerusalem and its surroundings, became centers of attraction and developed elaborate out-of-door festivities, with stately processions, to celebrate incidents from Jesus' life and triumph. These ceremonies were then copied and disseminated by the pilgrims throughout Christendom. When it later became too difficult for Western pilgrims to go to Jerusalem, shrines in Rome associated with the martyred Peter and Paul became something of a substitute.

It was in the historical setting of Jesus' life in the Holy Land that a new approach developed to the celebration of the redemptive events: they were now seen from a *historical* perspective. Instead of a unitive paschal festival as before, there appeared separate commemorations of the different events which happened during the last part of Jesus' earthly life and afterwards. Other holy days emerged: the Sunday before Easter, later called Palm Sunday, to commemorate Jesus' triumphal entrance into Jerusalem; Maundy Thursday,[16] to recall the institution of the Last Supper and Jesus' washing of the disciples' feet; Good (meaning "God's" in old English) Friday, to reenact symbolically the rejection and crucifixion of Jesus; Holy Saturday, to pause at His tomb; Ascension Day, to follow the Lord to Mount Tabor, the presumed mount of the Ascension; and the Day of Pentecost, to remember the descent of the Spirit.

Instead of celebrating redemption primarily as a present reality experienced by the believers here and now, it was now the past events which were being primarily recalled in their historical detail. This, of course, led to a rich flowering of the liturgical calendar.

The 4th century added to the Christian calendar the celebration of January 6 as the Feast of the Manifestation (Epiphany) of God in Christ, and of December 25, which became our Christmas. As was noted before, early Christians did not celebrate Jesus' birth. The date of it was unknown, and the early church was not concerned about it. It celebrated the gift of redemption, not historical occurences of the past. However, as both January 6 and December 25 were popular pagan festivals associated with the birth of deities, the church needed to create its own holy days on those dates to wean the masses away from the heathen celebrations. As we have seen, January 6 was a great feast day in the East, and December 25 in Rome. Both were identified with the "birth (return) of the sun." Thus Christians in the East began to celebrate the birthday and manifestation of "the Sun of the world," Jesus Christ, on January 6, whereas Christians in Rome celebrated on December 25. On January 6 Eastern Christians celebrated also the manifestation of Christ's glory in the baptism of Jesus and in the miracle at Cana, where Jesus turned water into wine. This was to counteract pagan festivals associated with the deities of water and wine.

Christian Rome borrowed January 6 from the Christian East and started celebrating the manifestation of Christ to the Magi on this day, while the Christian East borrowed December 25 from the West for the Nativity of Christ, keeping January 6 primarily for commemorating Jesus' baptism. His birth ceased to be celebrated on that date, to avoid giving the impression that His "birth" as the Son of God coincided with His baptism, a view advocated by heretical teachers who claimed Jesus was only *adopted* as the Son of God. However, among Eastern Christians January 6 is still a much more important festival than among Western Christians.

In both East and West the church also developed a time of preparation for Christmas, our *Advent,* in analogy to the preparation for Easter. Thus a second season was added to the calendar, the *Christmas season,* lasting from the beginning of Advent, through the time after Epiphany, until the beginning of the paschal season.

The rest of the year was dotted by the days of martyrs and eventually also by other saints' days. The major saints' days came to provide convenient divisions for the summer and autumn seasons, such as the time after Sts. Peter and Paul (June 29) and the time after St. Lawrence (August 10). The entire year re-presented the drama of salvation and of the lives of the saints in whom Christ was glorified.

DEVOTION TO THE SAINTS

Devotion to the departed saints is as old as the story of their martyrdom. Their gallant fight and moral victory over their persecutors and over death could not but establish them as heroes of the church and as special friends of Christ, to whom they had remained faithful unto death. They were believed to have been given a special gift of the Spirit which enabled them to bear witness before their pagan enemies (Mark 13:11). Whereas other departed might have to wait for their awaking from the sleep of death until the final resurrection, the martyrs were surely united with God right upon their death and lived in intimate proximity to God (Revelation 6:9-11). Since they went through so much suffering and were so close to Christ, they were sure to understand the trials and tribulations of their brothers on earth and would pray to God for them, as Christians pray for each other also in this life. And, because "the prayer of a righteous man has great power" (James 5:16), their intercessions would surely be of great effect. Thus the martyrs and eventually also the "Mother of God" and other holy men and women, even the angels, emerged as the intercessors of the people of God before His heavenly throne. Their relics, that is, their earthly remains and the objects they used, were treasured. Their tombs and the other sites connected with them became places of pilgrimage, and their heroic figures became objects of sacred art.

The Christological development of the 5th century [17] gave rise to a great devotion to Mary as the "Mother of God." She who was the link between humanity and divinity in the drama of the Incarnation—she provided the Lord with His humanity and made a human Savior a possibility—came to be seen as the mother and kindly intercessor of all Christians. The new Christological emphasis on the reality of the Incarnation brought with it a new accent on the "Mother of God," and churches began to be built in her name. One of the councils dealing with the Christological controversies met in Ephesus in 431 at the first church we know to have been dedicated in her name. The famous church of St. Maria Maggiore of Rome, with its splendid mosaics, was erected in the next decade.

CHRISTIAN ART

The early Christians met for their services almost always in private houses. Sometimes when a house was donated for the exclusive use of the Christian community, they transformed the interior of the building adapting it for its new function as a meeting place for Christians. Because the persecution of Christians involved a wholesale destruction of church property in A. D. 303-4, only one example of such a house-church has survived. Archeologists discovered it in Dura-Europos at the caravan road in the Syrian desert. The building was preserved whole because it had become buried by a landslide, together with the city, when the city walls were battered by enemy troops in 256. As in the case of the Italian Pompeii shaken by an earthquake and then buried by volcanic ashes, the entire town simply sank underground as the city walls caved in. The church had been built only a few years before. The building was divided into two rooms: one large room for common meals, without any wall decorations, and a small room which served as a baptistry. The baptistry has a tublike baptismal font surmounted by a beautifully painted vault representing the evening sky. Both the vault and the adjacent wall are decorated with symbolic paintings.

The figures speak a sign language to those who are being baptized and to those who are witnesses of it. There are the representations of Adam and Eve, the Good Shepherd, the forgiveness and healing of the paralytic, Jesus rescuing Peter walking toward Him on the water, the Samaritan woman at the well, David and Goliath, and a highly symbolic picture of the night of the Resurrection: Christ's grave, still closed, and the three Marys moving toward the grave with torches and vases of myrrh.

The only other significant deposit of early Christian art is in the catacombs, the underground cemeteries found in Rome, Naples, Sicily, France, Greece, and the Near East. The catacombs are subterranean passages, often dug several stories deep, with tombs on both sides of the passage. The latter opens out into the chapel-like recesses, where small groups could meet for prayer. People from the East were always used to burying their dead in caves, and the catacombs were artificial substitutes for caves. Families and friends met there to remember the dead. Contrary to popular belief, Christians did not meet in the catacombs for their regular worship; the open spaces there would have been too small for that. They met in catacombs primarily to celebrate the triumph of their brethren, especially of the martyrs, over death. In their underground cemeteries they could do this without fearing detection.

The walls of the catacombs are witnesses to the faith of the early church, showing also how the faith was expressed in ways which would be meaningful to the men and women of the time. Their exceedingly simple line drawings were for the most part not done by professional artists; they were not intended to convey aesthetic pleasure but a coded message. The church took over pre-Christian symbols frequently and filled them with Christian meaning. Well-known pagan and Old Testament figures were chosen to communicate Christian faith and hope. So the representation of the Good Shepherd is patterned on the shepherd figure of Hermes, the ancient messenger of the gods. Christ is on catacombs walls there in the guise of a philosophy teacher or as the sun-god Helios in his celestial chariot, for Christ is both the Teacher of heavenly wisdom and the Light of the world. Old Testament scenes outnumber the scenes from the New Testament, but it is the Gospel to which they bear a veiled witness: Noah's ark represents the waters of Baptism (1 Peter 3:20 ff.); David and Goliath speak of Christ vanquishing Satan; Jonah and the great fish testify to Jesus' death and resurrection ("the sign of Jonah," Matt. 12:39 ff.); the rock which gave forth water as Moses struck it with a wand stands for the quenching of spiritual thirst through the Eucharist. (1 Cor. 10:1-4)

Of the New Testament scenes the raising of Lazarus, the symbol of the resurrection of the faithful, is the favorite. The Nativity and the Crucifixion are not presented. The art is symbolic, not narrative or realistic, and so the hastening of the Magi or the baptism of Christ, who is portrayed as a little boy, replaced the actual Nativity scene. A basket of loaves and fishes, doves pecking at grain or grapes, or Christ feeding the multitude stand for the Eucharist. A ship, or Noah's ark, symbolizes the church as it sails the stormy sea of life, bound for the safe haven above. The anchor represents the ship's stability and thus hope. The dead buried in the catacombs are pictured with hands raised in prayer, as if taking part in a priestly service. The walls also bear various inscriptions and symbolic designs, such as the cross in the form of an anchor, monograms of *Je*sus *Chr*ist (which in Greek letters is IH XP), and the famous symbol *ICHTHYS*, the Greek word for "fish," composed of the initials of *Je*sus *CH*rist, Son of God, Savior. The ancients believed that fish never slept, and so the fish became also the symbol of the ever watchful and caring God.

Once Christianity became legal, large buildings were given by the emperor and other prominent Christians to the church. They were the basilicas, the name used for Roman public buildings, such as courts of justice or market halls. Interestingly enough, the architecture of the temples was not imitated. The early basilicas were rectangular and offered ample space for the huge assemblies at Christian services and for the living quarters of the clergy. Unlike the temples, they were entirely enclosed and had an inconspicuous exterior. Large squares in front offered room for the crowds and for the clergy processing from one church to another.

One enters a basilica through a narthex, or enclosed porch. The body of the basilica consists of a nave, flanked by aisles and a semicircular apse in front, the place for the holy table [18] and clergy. Columns, separating the aisles from the nave, carry an A-shaped roof. The inside of walls and roof is brightly painted and carries mosaics. There are many windows. As there is no stained glass, the interior is filled with light. In the East basilicas have vaulted roofs; they are more magnificent and their columns carry profuse ornamentations. After Constantine's time the ground plans of the basilicas became more complicated and could even be round or octangular, calling for many-domed roofs.

The mosaics in basilicas were composed of brightly colored stones and cubes of glass. Often set in the floors, they took the place of decorative carpets. In addition to portraying representations of the apostles and martyrs, and eventually of the "Mother of God," they continued to use traditional pagan and Christian themes. However, the art was now highly skilled and professional. It became simply resplendent under Byzantine-Oriental influence. The whole basilica was dominated by the icon, or picture, of *Christus Pantocrator,* Christ the Ruler of all, placed high on the wall of the apse. The pictures were stylized and majestic inspired by imperial art and ceremonial. They conveyed the idea of the church as a reflection of the court of heaven.

Notes

1. See Ambrose, *The Sacraments*, V:24 ff., where Ambrose discusses the petition "Give us this day our daily bread," referring it, as was customary, to the Eucharistic nourishment. For the transl. of the text see *St. Ambrose, Fathers of the Church*, Vol. 44, ed. R. J. Deferrari (Washington, D. C.: Catholic University Press, 1963), pp. 317 ff.
2. Ibid., 6:1 (p. 319) and 5:17 (p. 314). See also Gregory of Nyssa, *Address on Religious Instruction*, 37, for the idea of the drink, in E. R. Hardy, *Christology of the Later Fathers, Library of Christian Classics*, Vol. 3 (Philadelphia: Westminster Press, 1954), p. 320.
3. The Eucharistic theology of the period under our survey is rather complex and somewhat diverse. For an extensive documentation and explanation of the terminology employed see J. N. D. Kelly, *Early Christian Doctrines*, 2nd ed. (New York: Harper & Row, 1960), pp. 211-16, 440, 455. Cyril of Jerusalem's catechetical lectures of the mid-4th century, *Mystagogical Catechesis* V:7 (see Appendix, No. 2, pp. 135 ff.), represents the teaching that the elements become the body and blood of Christ by the invocation *(epiclesis)* of the Holy Spirit. St. Ambrose's catechetical lectures in *The Sacraments*, IV.4:14, 19; IV.5:23; VI.1:3 (op. cit., pp. 302, 304, 305, 319), lay stress on the transforming efficacy of the words of Christ.
4. St. John Chrysostom, *In Tim. hom.* 15,4 as transl. in Kelly, op. cit., p. 450, and St. Gregory of Nyssa, op. cit. 37, p. 321.
5. St. Ambrose, op. cit. IV:24, p. 305.
6. St. Cyril of Jerusalem's *Mystagog. Catechesis* IV:3, in *Lectures on the Christian Sacraments*, ed. F. L. Cross, tr. R. W. Church (London: SPCK, 1960), p. 68.
7. The Eucharistic prayers follow a fixed pattern and so their greater part is called the "canon," that is, the "unchanging rule." Technically, the canon begins only after the Sanctus (the "Holy, Holy, Holy"), as this is a late addition to the Eucharistic liturgy. The canon is introduced by the Preface, which begins with the Eucharistic Dialogue. (See pp. 33 f.)

8. Ambrose, op. cit., II.7:23, p. 287, and Cyril of Jerusalem, op. cit., II:4, p. 61, respectively.
9. For the meaning of the anointings see Walter Oetting, *The Church of the Catacombs* (St. Louis: Concordia Publishing House, 1964), p. 30.
10. Ambrose, op. cit., III:2 and 3, p. 290.
11. John Chrysostom, *Baptismal Instructions* IX:20, *Ancient Christian Writers*, Vol. 31, ed. P. W. Harkins (Westminster, Md.: Newman Press, 1963).
12. For details see also Oetting, pp. 72-4.
13. 1 Corinthians 5:5-6.
14. Ezekiel 3:16-18 and 33:1-9.
15. The reason why Jewish and Christian Passover celebrations often do not coincide in time is that there are different ways of calculating the spring equinox.
16. "Maundy" may come from the Latin *mundare*, to wash. Some derive it from *mandatum*, command, in view of our Lord's words in John 13:34.
17. See the section, "The Mystery of the Person of Christ," in the next chapter.
18. The word "altar," probably related to the Latin *altus*, high, designates something elevated. It is not derived from the word for the sacrificial altar of paganism. The altar was a freestanding table, usually with the bishop's chair behind it. The ancient tradition was for the teacher to be seated. The chair (*cathedra* in Greek, *sedes* in Latin, from which come such expressions as "cathedral" for the bishop's church and holy "see" for the papal office) became the symbol of the teacher's authoritative office. The bishop taught his congregation from his chair. There were no pulpits and pews in ancient church buildings. The interior of a basilica was spacious and unclogged.

3.

FAITH AND TEACHING

THE CORE

The center of Christian life was the faith that Jesus Christ provided a new life and gave power over evil and death. Those who joined the early Christian community through Baptism found their lives transformed and the power over evil and death broken. Cyprian of Carthage, for example, wrote:

> I used to regard it as difficult in respect of my character at that time, that a man should be capable of being born again. . . . 'How,' said I, 'is such a conversion possible, that there should be a sudden and rapid divestment of all which, either innate or hardened in us . . . has become inveterate by long accustomed use? . . . I used to indulge in my sins as if they were actually parts of me and indigenous to me. . . . But after that, by the help of the water of new birth, the stain of former years had been washed away, and a light from above, serene and pure, had been infused into my reconciled heart. . . . Then, in a wondrous manner . . . what before had seemed difficult began to suggest a means of accomplishment, what had been thought impossible to be capable of being achieved.[1]

Thus the teaching of the ancient church was based not only on Holy Scripture but also on the experience of deliverance, or salvation, which Christ brought to mankind. The core of Christian theology was Christology.[2] Its basis was soteriology, *soteria* meaning "salvation," or "deliverance," in Greek.

This explains the puzzling fact that the theological struggles in the 4th and 5th centuries, the centuries which worked out the great creeds of Christendom, were largely Christological. This was the question theologians as well as the people asked: "Who was and is this Christ who brought us a new life, who brought us from darkness into light, the Christ whom we worship?" Theology at this time was also a consuming concern of the laymen, educated and uneducated, and not just of the clergy. One of their concerns may be stated thus: "We worship but one God, and yet our worship is Christ-centered. How do we reconcile the apparent contradiction? Do we worship two divine beings, after all?" The ancient theologians wrestled with this problem because they knew that the community's life of prayer is the yardstick of its belief.[3] Christian worship finds its focus in two acts, Baptism and Communion, both centered in Christ. One is the beginning of the life in Christ and the other its nurture. What are the implications of this for theology?

THE MEANING OF REDEMPTION

The early Christians viewed Baptism as the birth to a new life, and the Eucharist mainly as the means of sustaining it. We can see from this that redemption was understood primarily as the victory of life over the powers of destruction and darkness. In his youthful writing *On the Incarnation*, St. Athanasius, the great theological teacher of the 4th century, explained that since life and the power over death are inherent in God alone, Jesus Christ, who lived a life victorious over death and gives a new life to people, must be God Himself present and active in the midst of men. In Him God and man, so long and so tragically separated by mankind's defiance or ignorance of God, are marvelously joined and mankind is plugged in on the Source of life again. This is the deepest meaning of the Incarnation, God's becoming "flesh" (*caro* in Latin), or man. What no man and no creature at all could accomplish, namely, the bridging of the wide gulf between man and God, God Himself undertook to accomplish by His becoming man in Jesus Christ.

The gulf between man and God has given rise to all the tragedies in mankind's history: man's enslavement to evil and his ultimate defeat by death. Therefore the union between God and man in Jesus brings also victory over the powers of evil and annuls the finality of death. Death is no longer the final word for man. *Christus victor:* Christ is victorious. The victorious Christ is the final word. For in Jesus' death the divine life inherent in Him overcame the powers of death as the rising sun vanquishes darkness. The process was already begun in Jesus' conflict with the powers of evil during His life. The victory was made manifest in Jesus' resurrection and became also the experience of the men and women who were instructed in the Christian faith and joined the Christian community. In Baptism they were united to God in Christ and filled with His Spirit. They lived a new life, and their union with God and their brothers was weekly renewed by their taking part in the banquet of Jesus Christ, the Holy Communion. All the world witnessed the power and life of God at work in this community. The power of the Resurrection was already evident in the healings which took place in the Christian church and in the martyrs' bold defiance of death. And since Christians had thus already a part in the divine life, as they were united to Him who triumphed over death, they too would be victorious over ultimate death. "*Who, then, can this life-giving, triumphant Christ be but God Himself* in the flesh of man?" they asked. This is how the Christian community saw it.

Christ as the victorious and reigning King was the central image of Jesus the Redeemer during this age as well as in the early Middle Ages. This is why the early crucifixes, once they appear on the scene (the first centuries did not produce crosses or crucifixes at all), have Jesus *reigning* from the cross, not hanging on it as a helpless, defeated victim. Other intriguing illustrations of the ancient Christian understanding of redemption are the "icons of the Resurrection," produced in the early Middle Ages and still made in Eastern Christendom. The actual resurrection is not their subject; they instead portray Jesus' victorious "Descent into Hades" (Hell), His "Harrowing of Hell."[4] The ancient pictures try to say in symbolic language what the theologians were saying in their teaching: *Jesus' death and resurrection are inseparable,* and in Jesus' death the resurrection was already in the making. The power and hold of death were broken by Christ's entering the realm of death (Hades); He was thus able to release men from the hold of death. The icons picture the gates of Hades thrown wide open. They show Christ with the victorious banner of the cross, and the dead, often headed by Adam and Eve, as finally free. Death or Satan is seen languishing under Christ's trampling foot. Jesus' own rising from the tomb is not portrayed; ancient Christian art shied away from realistic or naturalistic representations. The idea represented in these icons is also contained in the somewhat puzzling clause in the Apostles' Creed: "He descended into Hades" (Hell) — to *conquer* it.[5] Early-medieval hymns are a telling expression that Jesus' apparent defeat, His death, was, paradoxically, a victor's feat: Jesus "as a victim won the day."[6]

This victorious faith proved the main attraction of Christianity during the era of its greatest expansion, its first thousand years.

CHRIST, THE REVELATION OF GOD

To ancient Christians Christ was first of all the Redeemer of men; but He was also the Revealer of God. It was their conviction that in Him the mind and will of God, His very being, are revealed, that is, unveiled.[7] The mystery of God's mind and being is so great that it transcends all human minds; man's reason cannot penetrate or explore it. The infinite and wholly transcendent God must come to man's aid if man is to know him. The knowledge of God can come only through God's self-disclosure. This is the Biblical assumption. No one but God's own mind knows God's mind. It follows that if Christ brings the knowledge of God to men, He must be, in some mysterious way, the mind of God Himself, the Mind, or *Logos* in Greek, by which God made the world and by which He ever reveals Himself to men. He is the wisdom of God that never changes and is from everlasting (Prov. 7:22-30). This is what the Gospel of John says, especially in its Prolog. (John 1:1-18)

The word which this Prolog uses in the Greek text is *Logos*, which can be translated as both "Mind" and "Word." It seems that both meanings are intended here; it is usually used by the ancient Greek Christian writers in this double meaning. God created the world by His *Logos*, and by it He enlightens all men. This *Logos* became incarnate in Jesus Christ, who is *the* self-expression of God.

The word *Logos* was a useful term for ancient theology, for it played an important role in Greek philosophy as well as in the Old Testament. To those trained in philosophy it meant before all else the Mind, the rational Principle inherent and discernible in the universe, the divine Intelligence which forms and governs the harmonious cosmos as well as all rational creatures. This concept was a bridge to the Biblical understanding of God, the Creator, who governs His world and reveals His will to men. The Hebrew Bible spoke of God's Word as the instrument of God's creation (God *said* . . . and it was so) and revelation, for when He *speaks* He reveals something of Himself and His will. His Word is His self-expression. When the Old Testament was translated into Greek, the translators made use of the term *Logos* to speak of God's Word. Thus a synthesis between the Hebrew and Greek worlds was created; the Bible now could speak to the Greeks. The Christian theologians who spoke of Jesus as the *Logos* of God could strike a familiar chord for both Jews and Gentiles and so communicate what the church meant by Jesus as the Revealer of God in terms meaningful to their world.

CHRIST AND GOD

The Ecumenical Creeds, the heritage of the greater part of Christendom, were hammered out in the heat of controversies about the relationship of Christ to God and to man. The Nicene Creed was shaped by the Arian controversy.

Arius was a presbyter in Alexandria in the early 4th century. For centuries Alexandria had been a center of Greek philosophical learning. Already before the Christian era the Jews who had settled there thought more often in philosophical than in Biblical categories or, rather, unconsciously read Greek philosophical concepts into the Bible. The pioneer of this process was Philo. The Greek-influenced Jewish thinkers were not aware of the profound differences between the philosophical and Biblical approaches to reality. The Greek-educated Christians continued in this tradition in varying degrees. Arius is its extreme product.

Arius taught that God is so transcendent that He Himself could not create the world or be in any way accessible. He saw an infinite gulf between God and all else, a gulf unbridgeable from either side. The idea of a chasm between the infinite and the finite and of the inferiority of everything finite was of Greek and Oriental philosophical origin. It had led the Gnostics to deny any connection between the High God and the world. Although Arius was not a Gnostic—he did not teach that matter was contemptible—he had a certain kinship with the Gnostics.[8] Arius used the Greek philosophical-Christian tradition that God created the world by means of the divine *Logos* (John 1:3) and claimed that God first created a being called "Logos" or "Son of

God" in order that this divine yet inferior and created spirit might make the world which God could not make without losing His deity. The servant-spirit created the world and eventually became incarnate in Jesus Christ. It was also this "Logos" that granted the divine revelations men received.

The last doctrine named above could be perfectly orthodox, for in the Christian tradition it was the *Logos*, or Word of God, which was the means of all revelation. But the relationship of the *Logos* to God was completely different in traditional Christian teaching from that expressed in the teaching of Arius. Arius denied any interior or essential relationship between God and the *Logos*. The agent of creation and of revelation was, according to him, not God's own *Logos* (Mind and Word) or Son *properly* so called, but something exterior to God and only *called* "Logos" or "Son." He was a separate being, divine or semidivine, but not something essential to the being of God nor an expression of God. For God's own mind cannot come into contact with the world, according to Arius. Therefore it can neither make it nor reveal itself to it. Even God's agent of creation cannot come into real contact with Him, cannot know Him. God is essentially beyond reach.

Arius ended up without knowing anything about the love of God that leads God into a relationship with the world and to dwell in it. As St. Gregory of Nyssa, the greatest theological mind of the Greek-speaking East, later pointed out, the Incarnation is not a loss of God's greatness; it *shows* the greatness of God, who was willing to stoop so low in order to save men.[9] Besides, there is nothing inherently inferior about the world, which God saw as "very good," according to the Bible (Gen. 1:31). Arius also ended up with two divine beings, one superior, one inferior, for to Arius the Father and the Son were not essentially one. With one foot Arius was still in the polytheistic world of ancient thought, and his ideas gave no difficulties to new converts from paganism, accustomed as they were to a multiplicity of gods and demigods. To Athanasius, who was then a young deacon in the church of Alexandria, the greatest problem with Arius' doctrine consisted in its threat to the security of salvation. For, if it was not the true God who became man in Jesus Christ, how could men receive divine life from Him? The Arian issue rocked the church.

Arius' doctrine became rather popular. He even composed popular musical hits to instill his teaching among the common people. Almost simultaneously with Constantine's rise to the imperial throne and the church's rise to imperial favor, the Christian church faced the danger of an imminent split over the Arian doctrine. Alarmed, Emperor Constantine immediately summoned a worldwide conference of Christian bishops, called the First Ecumenical Council, or Synod,[10] to Nicaea (Iznik in today's Turkey), near his imperial residence in Nicomedia. This Council, meeting in 325, was an important watershed in the history of the church. It was the first time an emperor called a Christian council. It was also the first gathering of Christian leaders beyond their regional boundaries. Before the legalization of the church, Christians could hardly undertake such a conference. There had been no organized body which could represent the whole church. Now the Christian churches could deliberate and agree on policies and principles of common interest to all.

The Nicene Council agreed on a creed for all the churches, the famous First Ecumenical Creed of Nicaea. Up to then each city or region had its own version of the baptismal creed. The various creeds followed a basically common pattern, a pattern best known to us from the Apostles' Creed.[11] The Nicene Creed, in an expanded form, has remained as the one truly ecumenical Christian creed to this day.

The creed accepted at Nicaea kept the usual structure of the ancient Christian creeds, narrating the events of creation and redemption. What the Council added was a precise metaphysical explanation of the relationship between Jesus Christ and God. It took a stand against the Arian position that the world was made and saved by someone different from God. The Council said: The world was made and redeemed by God by means of His Son, who is an expression of God. Its Creed affirmed the unity between the *Logos* and God. The crucial anti-Arian affirmations in the Nicene Creed are: "We believe in one God . . . Maker of all things visible and invisible, and in . . . Jesus Christ, begotten uniquely of the Father, that is, of the substance of the Father, God of God, Light of Light, true God of true God, begotten, not made, of one being [essence, or substance] with the Father, through whom all things came into being . . . who for us men and for our salvation came down and was incarnate, becoming man."

The Nicene Creed was originally in the plural. It expressed the corporate faith of the church. The Creed insisted that the Son of God is the "true God," "of one being with the true God," and not another being separate from God. The relationship of the divine Son to His Father is seen like that of a light (flame) lit from a light; they are not different from one another, although one is generated from the other. The Father is the source of the Light, which is Christ. The Son is not a creature, someone made by God, as Arius had claimed, but is "begotten," or "generated," by the Father, though not in a physical manner. The difference between God's creature and God's Son is analogous to the difference between an artist's sculpture and his child; only the latter is of the "substance" of the father, bearing his life in him. The phrase "of one being ["of the same substance"] with the Father" was considered the most crucial in the argument with the Arians, who wanted "of similar being" [substance] or "of like being" in its stead. The Nicene Creed affirmed the identity of the Father's and the Son's essence, or of the underlying reality behind the Father and the Son, for the Son is an expression of the Father. He is the Word "through whom all things came into being."

We should notice the soteriological climax of the affirmations about the true divinity of Christ: ". . . who for us men and for our salvation . . . was made man." It is because of this that the foregoing is important. The Nicene theologians were not concerned with some abstruse speculations about matters which had no connection with the human situation. The eternal status of the Messiah was important to them because men needed such a great Redeemer if they were to be delivered from their alienation from God and from their consequent captivity by the forces of evil and death.

The struggle with Arianism was by no means ended by the Nicene Council's acceptance of the anti-Arian credal formulation. The Arian forces soon recovered. More than 50 years of warfare followed between the Arian and Nicene parties. Since the unity of the empire was threatened by the splitting of the church, the emperors and their imperial politics became deeply involved in the struggle. The principal means of coercion used by pro-Arian and anti-Arian bishops, councils, and especially by emperors, who simply wanted peace at any price, were excommunication, deposition from ecclesiastical office, and the sending of bishops into exile by the emperor. Athanasius, who became bishop of Alexandria shortly after the Council of Nicaea and was Nicaea's chief theological defender, was excommunicated, deposed, exiled, and then again restored many times during his long battle-filled life (he died in 373). He spent most of his career in exile or even in hiding. Many attempts at compromise between the Arian and Nicene theologians were framed, but none of them worked out. The Nicaean side finally won the empire by a combination of hard theological work, shrewd politics, and the arrival of the theologically well-informed, pro-Nicene Theodosius upon the imperial throne in 380. He summoned an "ecumenical council" to Constantinople the next year, and this council reaffirmed the Nicene formula that the Son is "of one being with the Father," or "of the same substance as the Father." It was this Council which apparently adopted the Nicene faith in its present credal form as used in the liturgy and confessional books of Christian churches all over the world.

FAITH AND TEACHING

THE HOLY SPIRIT

The original Nicene Creed was reserved about the Holy Spirit, since the status of the Holy Spirit was not at stake in the early stage of the Arian controversy. Thus the Creed simply said, "And [we believe] in the Holy Spirit." As the century proceeded, the situation changed. It became necessary to think through and state the relationship of the Spirit to God after some stated that the Holy Spirit is simply a supreme angelic creature. Athanasius wrote that if the Holy Spirit has the power to join men to God, as Christians believed happened in Baptism, then the Holy Spirit has to be the Spirit of God Himself. Such a task, he reasoned, could no more be accomplished by a creature than could man's redemption.[12] St. Basil the Great, the leader of the Nicene party after Athanasius, picked up the thread where St. Athanasius had left off and pointed out that in the liturgy, the yardstick of the church's beliefs, the Spirit is invoked and adored in the same breath as God the Father and God the Son. Since the church worships only God, the Holy Spirit must belong to God as intimately as does Jesus Christ.[13] Or else, why do Christians baptize "in the name of the Father and the Son and the Holy Spirit"?

Because of this controversy, the Council of Constantinople added a paragraph about the Holy Spirit to the Creed. Yet in comparison with the lengthy and complex Christological part of the Creed, the wording about the Holy Spirit is reserved and modest; it does not attempt to define or explain the Spirit. The divine nature of the Holy Spirit is stated in the Creed, just as in the New Testament, only indirectly: by the references to the divine origin and work of the Holy Spirit and by the references to the church's worship. In a way, all the following affirmations in the Creed are statements about the work of the Holy Spirit: "And [we believe] in the Holy Spirit, Lord and Lifegiver, coming [proceeding] from the Father,[14] worshiped and glorified with the Father and the Son, [the Spirit] who spoke through the prophets; and in the one, holy, catholic[15] and apostolic Church; we confess one Baptism for the remission of sins, and we look forward to the resurrection of the dead and the life of the age [world] to come." The stress on the activity of the Spirit, rather than on who or what the Spirit is, was not only Biblical; it reflected the experience of the Christian community, which was very conscious of the animating Breath[16] of God in its midst. In the ancient era Christians were much more aware of the role of the Spirit than Christians in a later era, especially later in the West.

THE MYSTERY OF THE TRIUNE GOD

As is apparent from the above, the church fathers were struggling with the mystery of the triune God, the one God who was known to the faithful as the Father in heaven, Jesus Christ the Redeemer, and the Holy Spirit. The anti-Arians fought first for the essential unity of the three. However, also the distinctness of the Father and the Son and the Spirit had to be maintained in order to be true to the Gospel record, which portrays Jesus as praying to the Father and promising His disciples to send them the Spirit. To express the divine unity, the church fathers spoke of the oneness of "being" (essence, or substance) shared by the divine Trinity.

To express the distinctness of the three, the theologians were driven to use perhaps more misleading terms, since no adequate words were available. Basil spoke of the three *hypostases*, a rather ambiguous and untranslatable word for that which exists in its own right and does not have a borrowed existence. The Latins either used the Greek word or spoke of the three "persons" of the Trinity.

It must be remembered, however, that the word *persona* in ancient Latin did not have the same connotation which the word "person" has acquired for us today. The word "person" was not conceived psychologically. Thus when the Fathers speak of the three "persons" of the Trinity they do not mean that there are three different personalities in God. Ancient philosophy was not concerned with the uniqueness of each individual but rather with that which the different individuals of the same species share in common, for example, what makes all men "human," or what makes tables "tables." The discovery of personality came only later, under Augustine, and was a result of Christian influence. But the new concept of "personhood" was not applied to the three "persons" of the divine Trinity.

Thus, while the Father, the Son, and the Spirit are distinct, they share the same divine nature and are one God. There is no adequate human vocabulary for the triune character of God. From the human perspective it has to remain a paradox. St. Augustine, in his monumental work *On the Trinity* in the early 5th century, finds an analogy for the triuneness of God in the triuneness of the human personality composed of "memory," "intelligence," and "will." As man is made in the image of God, his inner being reflects in an imperfect way the Holy Trinity. If it were not for his Fall, man's faculties and actions would be as perfectly integrated as the being and the work of the Holy Trinity, for God is no split personality. The triunity of God transcends the comprehension of man. It is a mystery apprehended only by faith.

THE MYSTERY OF THE PERSON OF CHRIST.

The 4th-century theologians wrestled primarily with the question of Christ's relationship to the Father. In the 5th and 6th centuries (as also in the 7th) theological struggles concentrated on the relationship of the divine and human in Christ's person, that is, on Christology. At stake here were the reality of Christ's humanity, the unity of His person, and the redemptive significance of both. Can one say that God the Word was born as human beings are? That He suffered privations, was limited in His knowledge, and died? How can the eternal and all-powerful God be born, have any weaknesses, and die? Isn't this contradicting the nature of God?

Several different answers were given. They were strongly influenced by the regional traditions of the different theologians. The theological school (tradition) of Alexandria in Egypt was characterized by Athanasius' stress on the saving significance of the full deity of Jesus Christ. The rival theological school of Antioch in Syria was preoccupied with the reality of Christ's humanity as the condition for His being able to redeem humanity. The West held to Tertullian's (turn of 3rd century) balanced stress on both aspects of Christ and did not indulge in much speculation on the subject.

The controversy started in the East already in the second half of the 4th century. An Alexandrian theologian named Apollinaris could not see how Christ could have both the Divine Mind and a human mind if He was one person, sinless, and a true Savior. Apollinaris concluded that Jesus was human as far as His flesh was concerned, but that in Him the Divine Mind (the *Logos*) replaced the fallible and sin-bent mind of men. The *Logos* even acted as the life-giving principle in Christ's flesh, forming one (divine-human) nature with it. This fusion of the *Logos* with the flesh made Christ's body life-giving. "The holy flesh is one nature with the Godhead, and infuses Divinity into those who partake of it [in the Eucharist]."[17] (We should note Apollinaris' characteristically Alexandrine use of the word "nature," by which was meant one entity or what we might call one "person." This is not how the word was used in Antioch.)

But was Christ, then, actually human when He lacked what makes man man: the human mind? So asked the Cappadocian church father Gregory of Nyssa.[18] The church, in a series of councils culminating with the Second Ecumenical Council (held in 381 at Constantinople) condemned Apollinaris' attempt to solve the Christological problem as creating an inhuman Christ. Apollinarianism was untrue to the Gospel record, which portrays Jesus as *"growing* in wisdom" (the Divine Mind certainly doesn't need to grow!), struggling with temptations, ignorant of the hour of the Kingdom's triumph, and crying on the cross, "My God, My God, why have You forsaken Me?"

It was not only faithfulness to the Biblical record which was at issue. The redemption of man as man was at stake, as the Cappadocian theologians pointed out. For, if man's salvation depends on God-and-man-becoming-one, and if Jesus is not fully man, then man is not redeemed. The Incarnation means that God assumed the entire human nature, including the mind of man. "By becoming exactly what we are, He united the human race through Himself to God." For, "what has not been taken up [by God] cannot be restored; it is what is united with God that is saved."[19] Since the emperor wanted an orthodox and united imperial church, Apollinarianism was outlawed by Theodosius. This did not mean, of course, that this kind of thinking simply died out. The controversy stimulated the church's leaders to think through some thorny questions. It took several centuries to tackle them. The Christological controversies finally resulted in a split of the church, a split which has lasted to this day.

The Antiochene school, as was already said, bent in the other direction than the Alexandrine. It was its great merit to insist on the importance and fullness of Jesus' humanity. It did not succeed at first to unite His humanity with His divinity in a satisfactory manner. The best-known but tragic product of the Antiochene Christological tradition was Nestorius, who became the imperial court preacher and patriarch of Constantinople in the first part of the 5th century. His Antiochene background, his coveted patriarchal rank, and his way of expressing his deep concerns made him almost an immediate object of attack by the Alexandrines. Alexandria was not only the chief rival of Antioch but also of Constantinople, which was considered the "New Rome" and therefore given higher ecclesiastical honor than the more ancient patriarchate of Alexandria.

For Nestorius, as for all Antiochene theologians, it was extremely important to keep the human and divine natures in Christ clearly distinct and not assign divine attributes to the former and human attributes to the latter. This was, however, customary both in the language of ordinary Christian piety and in the Alexandrine theology. So people spoke of Jesus' mother as the "Mother of God." To Nestorius this was outrageous, for how could God, who is without beginning, have a mother? His complaint seemed a justifiable one to ears unaccustomed to this title. But to popular piety Nestorius' storming against this usage seemed blasphemy. To the Alexandrines it was a clear sign that the new patriarch of Constantinople was, as could be expected, a heretic. For, wasn't Mary the mother of the Word-become-flesh? Nestorius would say that Mary was the mother of the man Jesus, but that it was nonsense to say that *God* was a small babe or that He, who is by nature immortal, died.

Cyril, the patriarch of Alexandria, challenged Nestorius as dividing Christ into two separate entities and denying the Incarnation. While Nestorius did not mean to deny the Incarnation, he could not, it seems, accept some of the basic consequences of this doctrine. In any case, his language certainly cast doubts on it. Reared in the Antiochene tradition, he was anxious to maintain the doctrine of the "impassibility of God," that is: God could not be subject to suffering *(passio* in Latin) or change. Speaking of God as subject to human experiences like birth and death was to him untrue to the nature of God. Yet if God became man, as Cyril pointed out, then it could and had to be said that He had a human mother, that He grew, and that He died, for this belongs to becoming man. Cyril and his school were anxious to maintain the unity of Christ's being. They said that in the Incarnation the divine and human natures became so indivisibly united that they came to form one, divine-human nature. To avoid splitting Christ into two entities and to maintain His integrity as a person, they liked to speak of the "one nature of the Incarnate God the Word,"[20] a complete union of the divine and human natures. These could be distinguished, at best, only in abstraction, they held, for Christ always acted as one person. To attribute His birth and death, for example, only to His humanity, and His supernatural powers only to His deity, would be to destroy the meaning of the Incarnation, the redemptive significance of the divine-human union in Christ, and the life-giving quality of the Eucharist, where the faithful received not just the body of a human Jesus.

The debate was conducted in a spirit of deepest distrust, hostility, and misunderstanding. Cyril, with his "one-nature" talk, sounded to Nestorius like an Apollinarian. He felt that in the Alexandrine theology, which attributed human characteristics to God and divine to the man Jesus, the Deity lost its real divinity and at the same time Christ's true humanity was destroyed. Cyril himself, on the other hand, was sure that Nestorius did not believe in Christ's deity, and he accused him of dividing Christ into two persons by his insisting on the "two natures" (divine and human) of Christ. He charged Nestorius with teaching that there were actually two Christs. The two schools of thought read different meanings into each other's terminology, and the fighting theologians often used hasty or intemperate language.

The controversies which arose were not only theological but also personal and political, as we have indicated. Regional and personal rivalries and the grossest of politics were involved. Thanks to Cyril's ruthless maneuvers, Nestorius lost his patriarchal position, was condemned by church councils, and was exiled by the emperor, Theodosius II.

Once his offensive rival was out of the way, Cyril and the Antiochene school came quickly to a mutual clarification of thought and language, arriving at an agreement called the Symbol of Union of 431. The Antiochenes were now willing to accept the title "Mother of God" *(Theotokos* in Greek) for Jesus' mother, and Cyril the expression the "two natures" as applying to the incarnate Lord. While the agreement was a great milestone in theological understanding, its binding force remained only as long as Cyril was alive (he died in 444). His more extreme partisans never really recognized it, being horrified by the "two natures" formula especially. To them it was an unworthy compromise, denying the complete union of the divine and human in Christ and, perhaps no less importantly, their distinct and treasured Alexandrine heritage. While Cyril himself came through the controversy to a greater appreciation of the importance of Jesus' humanity, some of his devoted disciples actually did lose from sight the fullness of Christ's humanity in their insistence on only the "one nature" of Christ. The result was a Christ in whom the human nature tended to be taken over by the divine. The "Monophysite" (from the Greek *monos*, "alone," and *physis*, "nature") Christ became in reality often only half-human. This, however, was characteristic of popular piety also in churches which did not hold to the "one nature" doctrine. Hebrews 2:16-17 was not too well absorbed by the mainstream of Christianity: "For surely it is not with angels that He is concerned but with the descendants of Abraham. Therefore He had to be made like His brethren in every respect, so that He might become a merciful and faithful high priest in the service of God, to make expiation for the sins of the people."

    Cyril's successor, the ruthless patriarch Dioscorus of Alexandria, succeeded in having the Symbol of Union annulled by what came to be known as the "Robber Council" of 449, ratified by the emperor but not recognized by the Roman pope. Yet a sudden change on the imperial throne (Theodosius fell off his horse and died) and the papal pressure for a fairer handling of the issues led to the summoning of the Fourth Ecumenical Council in 451. It met, for the convenience of the emperor, in Chalcedon and has gone down in history as rivaling only Nicaea in importance.

    The Council, acting under heavy imperial and papal pressures, approved "the letters of Cyril to Nestorius" and rejected both the Monophysite and Nestorian formulas. It accepted a doctrinal formulary called the "Tome of Leo," which had been sent by Pope Leo as a definition of the traditional faith of the church regarding the relationship of the divine and human natures in Christ. The Council tried to unite the different factions of Christendom by taking and uniting the best from all the three sides involved in the controversy (Antioch, Alexandria, and the West). The credal definition formulated at Chalcedon incorporated fragments from Cyril, the Symbol of Union (which had originated in Antioch), and Leo. Chalcedon affirmed the abiding reality of both the divine and human natures in Christ and the perfect union of the two in His person. It stated that on account of this it is possible, orthodox, and even necessary to say that Mary became the "Mother of God," since God became man and men have mothers, and also that God, while by nature immortal, could as *man* actually die. Moreover, the Lord Christ possessed not only the divine Mind as God but also a truly human mind ("the rational soul") as man. He became in all things like His brothers except for sin. His two natures had to be kept distinct (for example, God as *God* did not die); yet they always acted in union with one another.

How the divine and human attributes such as power and weakness, which contradict each other, coexisted alongside one another without canceling each other out was not explained. The mystery of the two natures of the one Christ was stated and left unresolved. It would have been a vain exercise had the Council attempted to resolve it. For the Chalcedonian formula that Christ is *"fully* God and *fully* man" cannot but remain an apparent contradiction, a paradox, a mystery found true only by faith. In this it corresponds to the paradox of the triunity of God.[21]

The great merit of the Chalcedonian Council was that it acknowledged both the genuineness and fullness of Christ's humanity and its indivisible union with His deity. It saw the mysterious union as the basis of the salvation of mankind. The Council's attempt at synthesis, however, did not heal the schisms and misunderstandings which rent the church with regard to the Christological question. The regional loyalties, the heavy hand of the imperial court that steered the Council and attempted to enforce, even by police measures, the Chalcedonian decisions, the semantic confusion over expressions like "two natures," popular emotion and conservatism involved in religion, and the lack of any outstanding theological leaders in the Chalcedonian camp in the East, all worked to undo the seeming accomplishment of the Council.

In time the school of Antioch seemed to have used up its light, and now the Monophysites provided the theological leadership. Most of the Monophysites, including their leaders, were actually perhaps no less orthodox than those who accepted the Chalcedonian definition. The picture was one of resentment and defensiveness rather than of deep theological differences. The imperial forces tried in vain to impose Chalcedonian "orthodoxy" on a discontented and aroused populace. For a century or so the fight continued within the officially one church of the empire of the East. The West had no trouble accepting Chalcedon. In the mid-6th century, however, the Monophysites, following the lead of Jacob Baradaeus and hence nicknamed "Jacobites," seceded from the imperial Byzantine, or "Greek-Orthodox," church and formed their own independent regional churches. Most Christians in Egypt and Ethiopia (the "Coptic," or "Egyptian" Christians), vast numbers in Palestine and Syria, the Syrian-planted "Mar Thomas" Church in South India, and the indigenous Church of Armenia became officially Monophysite, though considering themselves Catholic and Orthodox. On the other hand, the "Nestorians" had been pushed out of the empire and spread as a separate church into Syrian regions beyond the imperial frontiers: to the Empire of Persia and eventually to China and India.

Although ecumenical contact has been made in recent times, the tragic schism has not been healed. It weakened the Christian presence in the East considerably. It was even one of the major causes of the rapid surrender of Syrian,

Palestinian, and Egyptian cities to the Islamic Arabic invaders in the 7th century, for there was little love for the dictatorial, "heretical" Byzantine government in these disaffected regions of the empire. The Muslims promised freedom to *all* Christians.

A significant accompaniment to and result of the Christological controversies was the high status accorded to Mary, the "Mother of God." Devotion to Mother Mary was already strong by 400. Both the Monophysite and the Chalcedonian theologies encouraged its growth. Where the divinity of Christ tended to swallow up Jesus' humanity, as in circles with Monophysite tendencies, there the Holy Mother became the human mediator between the majestic Lord Christ and the human family. This was not confined to circles which were officially Monophysite, for the humanity of Christ tended to get lost to the sight of even "orthodox" believers, as we have seen.

The Chalcedonian theology, with its stress on Jesus' mother as the guarantor and bearer of Christ's humanity, likewise encouraged devotion to her. She became the link between man and God, because it was through her that God assumed human stature. She was thus made to be of saving significance to Christians, for had it not been for her there would have been no incarnation and therefore no redemption. Churches started to be named in her honor at the height of the Christological controversies in the early 5th century. It should be remembered that her importance in Christian devotion, however late it may have developed, was most intimately linked with the development of classical Christology and soteriology. Thus we end on the same note as we began: Christian theology and devotion are at their core Christological and soteriological, and they are inseparable from one another. Indeed, the devotion to the "Mother of God" and to her infant Son toppled Nestorius from his pulpit, for the faithful were enraged to hear that God could not be called a Babe in the arms of Mother Mary. The formula: Christ is "fully God and fully man" prevailed.

NORMS OF DOCTRINE

What were the norms by which a theological position was judged and considered orthodox and normative? From our discussion so far several norms have emerged. First, we pointed out that there was the norm given by the community's life of prayer—the *lex orandi lex credendi* principle. A theology had to be in harmony with the church's worship and devotion. Second, though not secondarily, the church's teaching had to conform to the basic credal tradition of the church and the experience of faith. Third, but certainly not third in importance, doctrine had to rest on Scriptural support, and that on clear, unambiguous passages in their *literal* meaning, concerning which there was a unanimity among the church's teachers.

A precise and definitive delimitation of the canon of Scripture—the determination of what belonged to it and what did not—did not occur until the 16th century, the time of the Reformation. The bulk of the New Testament books had been agreed upon already by around A.D. 200, but uncertainty about a few of the epistles and about the Book of Revelation remained for some time. By the 6th century most Christian churches used the same New Testament as we do today. The Old Testament in Greek was very naturally taken over from the Greek synagog at the start of the church's mission among the Greek-speaking population. This version of the Old Testament, as well as the Latin translations based on it, included books which were not in the Hebrew (and later in the Protestant) canon: the so-called Apocryphal books. In the 16th century the Protestant Reformers ruled that only the books from the Hebrew Scriptures belonged to the canonical Old Testament. The Counter-Reformation Council of Trent ruled that the Apocrypha belong to the canon and that they are binding for doctrine.

Three bases were used to determine whether a book should be included in the New Testament: its apostolicity, its orthodoxy, and its universal acceptance by Christian churches for use in public worship. Apostolicity meant that a book had to have direct or indirect apostolic origin in order to qualify for the New Testament. This was an important reason why the Epistle to the Hebrews and the Revelation to John, among others, had a hard time getting into the canon, for their apostolic origin was questioned by many. However, also the orthodoxy of these books had been questioned, since Hebrews stated that there was no forgiveness for a voluntary falling away from the faith (10:26-31), and yet the church admitted renegades to repentance. Revelation seemed to teach bewildering things about the return of Christ to the earth. (Rev. 20:1-10)

It is interesting to note that inspiration was not among the criteria which decided the canonicity of a book. Of course a book had to be inspired by God to be included in the Bible. Yet there were many other books which were considered inspired by God but which were not in the canon. They were thought useful for private reading and edification, but were not considered "canonical." A book belonged to the canon if it was used in public worship and for determining the church's doctrine. The word "canon" means a yardstick, or a ruler, in Greek. The canon of Scripture was to serve as a yardstick of the church's teaching. Thus Scripture had to have a *delimited* scope, while inspired literature could be unlimited. A canonical book could not have a private character, but it had to be universally known and recognized by all Christians. Since Scripture served as an authoritative basis for distinguishing between true and false teaching, its contents had to have a public character.

The Bible could be interpreted by at least three different methods: the literal, the typological, and the allegorical. The last two were especially used for the Old Testament, to show its abiding relevance. Typology saw various Old Testament events and figures, such as the liberation from Egypt, the Passover, and Moses, as types or figures of man's deliverance and life in Christ, which they foreshadowed. We noted this in the discussion on

Christian art. Allegory saw symbolic spiritual significance in the seemingly mundane or dated details of Biblical events and laws. The allegorical interpretation flourished especially in the theological school of Alexandria, where it had already been applied to the Old Testament and to Greek myths before the Christian era. Both the typological and the allegorical interpretations were already occasionally present in the New Testament, as in 1 Corinthians 10:1-6 and 9:8-11. The literal, historical interpretation was cultivated in the school of Antioch. Its greatest product in the art of preaching was John Chrysostom.

Since Scripture lends itself in many places to varied interpretations, it was felt that the church could not use only Scripture. This is why the church's basic and universal credal tradition and its formulation in the ecumenical councils served as a guide to interpreting Scripture where it appeared obscure, ambiguous, or as containing contradictions. Thus the church's living tradition of faith and worship was regarded as checking a possibly imbalanced, provincial, arbitary, or subjective interpretation of the church's holy books. As St. Vincent of Lerins put it in the early 5th century, "In the catholic Church every care should be taken to hold fast to what has been believed *everywhere, always* and *by all.* This is truly and properly 'catholic' . . . which comprises everything truly universal. This general rule will be truly applied if we follow the principles 'universality, antiquity and consent' . . . of all or almost all the bishops and teachers in antiquity."[22]

By "tradition" we mean the heritage of faith and worship which has been passed on from one generation to another and which creates the link binding all generations into an organic spiritual unity and giving the community its identity. Such a tradition in the ancient church was never set over and against Scripture, but was seen as identical with the faith of the Scriptures themselves. As we have seen, it was also not set against development. But growth in theology had to be harmonized with the ancient heritage.

FAITH AND TEACHING

Notes

1. *Ad Donat.* 3 f., trans. J. G. Davies, *The Early Christian Church* (New York: Holt, Rinehart & Winston, Inc., 1965), p. 128.
2. The teaching about or knowledge of Christ.
3. Based on the famous Latin saying, *Lex orandi, lex credendi,* which means literally, "The law of praying is the law of believing."
4. *Hades* in ancient Greek, as *sheol* in ancient Hebrew, was the mysterious realm of death (and of the dead), or the underworld. While it should not by any means be simply equated with hell (which is *gehenna* in New Testament language), it came to be thought of as the realm over which Satan held sway, the reign of death and the reign of Satan being almost synonymous. So the underworld eventually came to be equated with hell. Thus, in the words of some of the later Fathers, "This Lion, that is Christ, of the tribe of Judah descended victoriously to hell, snatching us from the mouth of the hostile lion." Again, "He descended to hell in order to rescue us from the jaws of the cruel dragon." Cited in John N. D. Kelly, *Early Christian Creeds* (London and New York: Longmans, 1952), p. 382.
5. For the history of this clause in the Creed see Kelly, pp. 378-83.
6. From the famous 6th-century hymn, "Sing, My Tongue, the Glorious Battle." It is interesting to note that Luther's Passion hymns, too, are simultaneously Easter hymns. So, for example, his "Christ Jesus Lay in Death's Dark Bands" *(Christ lag in Todesbanden).*
7. The English word "revelation" comes from the Latin for "unveiling." Its root is *velum,* or a veil.
8. See Oetting, pp. 54-56, for the teachings of the Gnostics.
9. *Address on Religious Instruction 27, Christology of the Later Fathers,* pp. 304 ff.
10. The word "ecumenical" comes from the Greek *oikoumene,* meaning the "whole inhabited world." The word "synod" is also from the Greek, and it means literally a "common way."

It was used for caravans and is a rather suggestive term for Christian gatherings.

11. The Apostles' Creed became the common baptismal creed of the West only in the Middle Ages, but is based on a very ancient Roman Christian creed. Its derivation from the apostles is a medieval legend. The Apostles' Creed is not used in Eastern Christendom. For the history of this creed see Kelly, op. cit., pp. 332-434.

12. "If the Holy Spirit were a creature, we should have no participation in God through Him; we should be united to a creature and alien from the divine nature. . . . If He makes men divine, His nature must undoubtedly be that of God." Athanasius, *Ad Serap.* 1, 27, as trans. in Kelly, *Early Christian Doctrines,* p. 258.

13. St. Basil: "That which is foreign in nature could not have shared in the same honors." *Ep.* 159, 2, as trans. in Kelly, *Early Christian Creeds,* p. 342.

14. The addition "and the Son" (*filioque* in Latin) was put in by later Western and anti-Arian churchmen. It was resented in the East as tampering with a venerable ecumenical creed.

15. From the Greek word *katholos,* literally, "according to the whole," meaning "comprehensive." Although the word has come to be translated primarily as "universal," its original meaning was apparently not geographic. It was a reference to the church which kept the faith according to the *whole* Gospel, in contrast to the heretics, who picked and chose from the Gospel what they pleased. When the meaning of the word "catholic" ceased to be understood in the West, it sometimes came to be replaced by "universal," "common," or "Christian" in the vernacular translations of the creed.

16. The word "spirit" means literally "breath" or "wind," with its life-giving, dynamic propelling power.

17. Cited in Kelly, *Early Christian Doctrines,* p. 295.

18. *Antiirrh.* 29:45; 23:33. See Kelly, op. cit., p. 296.

19. Gregory of Nyssa, *C. Eunom.* 12, and Gregory of Nazianzen, *Ep.* 101, 7, cited in Kelly, op. cit., p. 297.

20. The "one nature" (*mia physis* in Greek) phrase used by Cyril was taken over by him from Apollinarian sources which he believed to have Athanasius' authority behind it. See Kelly's op. cit., p. 319, especially n. 3, for some of the references to Cyril's usage of the formula.
21. See previous section, "The Mystery of the Triune God."
22. Cited from Vincent of Lerins, *Commonitories*, in *The Fathers of the Church*, Vol. 7, ed. R. E. Morris (New York: Fathers of the Church, Inc., 1949), p. 26.

4.
STRUCTURE, LEADERSHIP, AND SERVICE

Like any community, the ancient Christian church was composed of different categories of members, depending on their responsibilities and corresponding burdens and honors. One group was the people, *laos* in Greek, from which come our words "lay" and "laity." The others were the leaders, or clergy, from the Greek *cleros*, which means elected or selected. The apostolic church, of course, did not sharply distinguish between laity and clergy, except to observe that certain ones among them were set aside for the ministry of the Word.

Baptized lay persons in good standing were considered members of the holy people of God, also regarded as the new Israel, the family of God. Theirs was the privilege of bringing an offering, a token of themselves, in the liturgy. For this reason they were often called "the offerers," which signified their priestly role before God. They could participate in the prayers of the faithful (particularly in the "Our Father"), in the exchange of the kiss of peace, and in Communion. They also took part in the election of the bishop. The electoral privilege was eventually withdrawn from them because of the interference of the nobles and kings with elections in the early Middle Ages. To wrest the elections from feudal and royal politics, the appointment of bishops in the West was eventually taken over by the pope, whose own election was in turn placed into the hands of electoral bishops, the cardinals.

A TEAM MINISTRY

The clergy under the bishop was usually divided into seven different ministerial orders, each order or office having its own dignity and responsibilities and forming with the others a team ministry headed by the bishop. The team included presbyters (Greek word for elders, and the root of our word "priest"), deacons, subdeacons (also deaconesses, or widows), lectors (readers of Scripture in the services), acolytes (the bishop's messengers), exorcists (who also doubled as catechists, since they were in charge of the catechumens), and doorkeepers (custodians). By the mid-3rd century the different ministries had come to be seen as having different degrees of dignity, the humbler offices becoming stepping-stones toward the "higher" offices.

To become a bishop, for example, one ought to have passed through the other ministerial grades. This procedure, a new concept in the Christian community, was an imitation of the Roman civil service, with lower offices being at the bottom of the career ladder. It was certainly a useful experience for a leader charged with oversight to have served in the various other offices first. But the new arrangement took away some of the integrity and dignity from the "lower" offices; one started to look at them as temporary stages in a "career." In the end the ascent became a purely ritual procedure. One simply went through the ordinations to the various ministries in order to qualify for a "higher" one, even if one never exercised them. An early and extreme example of this was Ambrose, the governor of Milan, who in the second half of the 4th century was in one night rushed through all the grades of the ministry simply in order to be ordained the city's bishop. Roman Catholic seminarians still receive the various ordinations today, a relic of the great variety of ministries which the church had once possessed but gradually lost as the ministry became concentrated in the office of priest and bishop alone. There are many attempts today to revive the diversity and team character of the church's early ministry.

THE PARISH

The focal point of both civil and church administration in the Roman Empire was the city with its surroundings. Here was the bishop's see,[1] or seat. The entire city was the "parish," served by the bishop's team. "Parish" is from the Greek word *paroikia*, a colony. Christians considered themselves God's colony, or commonwealth, planted in this world. The citywide parish served by a team ministry meant a cooperative Christian venture, a division of labor according to various present needs and talents, and a pooling of all resources.

The appearance of the rather autonomous *local* parish in our sense of the word came only during the 6th and 7th centuries in the West. With the cities destroyed, the population was scattered across the countryside. The bishop's area of responsibility now became a huge rural area, too spread-out to be served by a mobile team ministry as before. The new conditions forced the bishop to appoint a resident presbyter (priest) to many of the outlying localities. The priest received his own small ministerial team to assist him. In consequence, the people of the locality they served became their parish, all the new parishes combining to make a loosely knit bishop's parish, the diocese. The rural presbyter was often more dependent on his local chieftain, noble patron, or abbot than on his bishop. He became, in a way, a small reproduction of the bishop to his people, that is, their pastor. Yet the bishop still kept a team for the work connected with his cathedral church and the nearby basilicas. The lowest (the "minor") three orders were now conferred on young boys who came to live as apprentices in the bishop's household, where they received their education for the church's ministry. The imperial schools had ceased to function in the barbarian lands of the West, and the church had to provide a substitute. The church had to be elastic and inventive in order to serve the changing world. Its cathedral schools were the embryos of future universities.

The strictly local semiautonomous parish, eventually served by only one minister, the priest, became finally the general church pattern and was retained even after modern industrialization created a new city civilization. Our cities and their suburbs are divided into hundreds and thousands of more or less independent parishes. This accounts in part for the unevenness of the services the church can provide to the different sections of the city. The ancient church was much more effective in the cities because its operations, actions, budgets, and ministries were a united venture of the entire Christian community of a city and its surroundings.

LEADERSHIP

What were the roles of bishops, presbyters, deacons, and those in female ministries? The bishop—*episcopos*, from the Greek word for "overseer" from which also "episcopal" and "episcopacy" are derived—was the chief pastor (shepherd) and leader of his people in matters spiritual and temporal. He was considered a successor of the apostles, which made him especially responsible for setting forth the Gospel. The bishop as guardian of the apostolic tradition, had to spread, preserve, define, and defend Christ's teaching. This made the bishop the authoritative teacher (*doctor* in Latin) and father of his people. The title "Father" was a term of filial reverence used for a teacher in the ancient world. The bishop was to ordain or set apart others for the church's ministry and to convey the Spirit by the laying on of hands on the newly baptized. A leader of a priestly people (Ex. 19:6 and 1 Peter 2:9), the bishop was a "high priest."

His actions at the altar of their earthly sanctuary mirrored to them the intercession and offering of Jesus, their "High Priest" in heaven. (Heb. 8:1). As the city's chief priest, the bishop presided over the Eucharistic celebration or delegated presbyters to do so if he could not be present. To preserve the sense of the church's unity in the large city of

THE CHURCH IN A CHANGING WORLD

Rome, the bishop consecrated a whole basketful of bread, of which a token piece was brought into each Christian assembly in the city.

As the leader of his "colony," the bishop, with the help of his presbyters, administered its financial operations, dividing its resources to maintain the poor as well as the church's clergy, buildings, and cemeteries. For this vast operation he used not only the services of the presbyters but also of his deacons and subdeacons, his widows and deaconesses. They were especially in charge of the poor, the sick, the widows, and the orphans and were the bishop's contact with the community. The Roman bishop had seven deacons, each in charge of one-seventh of the citywide parish. The deaconesses and widows were in charge of the women and children.

The budget of the ancient bishop was large. Many Christians were generous, and there were some wealthy and even regal donors. The people gave money or goods in kind, erected or donated basilicas, and bequeathed to the church great tracts of land. The church carried out a complex relief and philanthropic work, for it was the only agency caring for the sick, the bereaved, the prisoners, and the travelers. It also redeemed captives and sometimes succeeded in finding work for the unemployed. When the civil administration collapsed in Rome, the church took over the government's vast feeding program of the poor. So Pope Gregory the Great (ca. A. D. 600) not only supervised free bread-and-soup lines in the streets of Rome but also organized a system of runners who brought hot food to the infirm in their homes. Bishops and abbots founded and maintained both complex and simple shelters for the sick, the homeless, the destitute, and the travelers, for whom there were no inns.

As successors of the apostles, bishops were the administrators of the keys of the kingdom of heaven (Matt. 18:19 and John 20:23) and so were the chief justices of their people. They were assisted in their judicial roles by their presbyters as fellow justices. The early Christians were warned not to bring their suits before the pagan courts but to settle their quarrels by themselves. (1 Cor. 6:1-6). As they considered the Roman punishments inhumane, they also protected their fellow believers from the police. So the church developed its own disciplinary and judicial system with its rules, or "canons" (canon law). As each region and each period developed its own, attempts were made to collect and unify them, that is, codify them. The councils of bishops frequently created such canons. They served as legislative bodies and superior ecclesiastical courts, deciding matters of regional or universal import. The canons governed the duties and conduct of Christian laity and clergy, as well as penalties due to offenders. The bishop, with his presbyters, decided the suits of his people, executed their testaments, administered the inheritance of Christian widows and orphans, and was in charge of the church's penitential discipline. Emperor Constantine gave imperial recognition to the bishop's jurisdiction over Christians. Imperial laws made the bishops the official protectors of the weak members of society, with the duty to denounce abuses of power to the appropriate imperial authorities. The bishops had access to the inaccessible and august emperor. In 530 the bishops were placed in charge of the entire fiscal operations of Byzantine cities, including the supervision of public works.

When the Roman administration collapsed in the West, many a bishop picked up the pieces and became in effect his area's governor. He negotiated the peace with barbarians threatening his city. So the diplomatic skill and persuasiveness of Leo the Great, bishop of Rome in the mid-5th century, saved Rome from devastation both by the dreaded Huns and the Vandals.

In addition to their public responsibilities, bishops and presbyters served their people by private pastoral care, as visitors of the bereaved and ill, as counselors, and as healers of conscience.

In describing the enormous problems confronting the bishop in his position and work, St. John Chrysostom explains

that in this ministry one is thrown to the wild beasts of
> wrath, despondency, envy, strife, slanders, accusations, falsehood, hypocrisy, intrigues, anger against those who have done no harm, pleasure at the indecorous acts of fellow ministers, sorrow at their prosperity, love of praise, desire of honor (which indeed most of all drives the human soul headlong to perdition), doctrines devised to please, servile flatteries, ignoble fawning, contempt of the poor, paying court to the rich, senseless and mischievous honors, favors attended with danger both to those who offer and those who accept them, sordid fear suited only to the basest of slaves, the abolition of plain speaking, a great affectation of humility, but banishment of truth, the suppression of convictions and reproofs, or rather the excessive use of them against the poor, while against those who are invested with power no one dare to open his lips.[2]

The demanding and complex responsibilities of bishops and of their assisting presbyters in Christianized Roman cities had the effect that the best men shied away from the office. They felt unequal to the overwhelming responsibilities. It became as difficult to capture qualified men for the episcopal office as it is difficult to find qualified and willing presidents for today's complex universities. Many parishes had to resort to ruse and to an actual capture of the promising but elusive candidates. Some of the most famous leaders of the church, such as Ambrose, John Chrysostom, Basil of Cappadocia, Gregory Nazianzus, Augustine, and Gregory the Great, attempted to avoid or escape the office but were pressed into the job. Some were even forcibly ordained. Since ordination was considered as constituting a divine call, they could not very easily decline after that. We have amusing and moving documents about the hide-and-catch games that went on and the anxieties which the awesome responsibilities of the sacerdotal office evoked in

STRUCTURE, LEADERSHIP, AND SERVICE

these reluctant heroes. Like many Old Testament prophets, they preferred the private life, not so much because they were irresponsible but because they were too responsible, one might say.

Of course, there were, on the other hand, men who were only too willing to receive the prestige and privileges of the episcopal chair, men who should have never assumed it. The bearer of the office had much power and was exempted by Constantine from the crushing imperial taxes. This lured many power seekers and tax evaders to be bishops. Later, in barbarian times, when the bishop often amounted to a secular ruler, lay nobles understandably vied for the office, to become unchallenged chieftains of their region. All this led to the result that the best bishops were as a rule recruited from the ranks of the monks. It is a curious paradox that some of the men who became the best leaders of the church in a bustling world should have come from the ranks of those who had attempted to retreat from it. In the Eastern churches of today most bishops are still monks.

THE LARGER BONDS

What was the relationship of bishop to bishop and parish to parish? Was there any external structure to foster the unity of the worldwide Christian movement? After the death of the apostles and their associates individual Christian communities were quite independent. Although there was no organization tying the different congregations together, there was consultation and cooperation between them and their leaders, especially with regard to common problems. Naturally, the leading Christian communities and their bishops exercised an influence on smaller churches or on those of more recent origin. The importance of the city in which the congregation was located and its historic Christian origin were the two most important factors determining the moral and eventually the jurisdictional authority of a particular Christian community and its bishop. If a church happened to be located in the capital *(metropolis)* of a province or if it could boast an apostolic connection in its origin, its bishop became a respected spokesman in the family of churches. Meetings (synods or councils) of the bishops of a region came to possess legislative authority for the churches involved. Following the pattern of civil administration, the metropolitan bishop, or archbishop, as he came to be called, developed into the authoritative head of the region by the early 4th century. Appeals could be made to him from the other parishes. He became responsible for filling episcopal vacancies and received the power of vetoing unworthy candidates for episcopal offices or deposing unworthy bishops in his province. He summoned and presided over the councils of his bishops and enforced their decisions.

Standing even above the metropolitans were the patriarch-bishops of the most important sees of Christendom. In the Roman Empire these were the sees of its four largest cities: Rome in the West, Antioch of Syria, Alexandria of Egypt, and eventually Constantinople in the East. Since Constantinople was the new capital of the empire, it came to rank immediately after Rome, "because it was the new Rome." This was bitterly resented by the more ancient sees. By the latter part of the 5th century most of the patriarchs claimed and often obtained jurisdiction over all the provinces in their areas. In the 5th century Jerusalem received patriarchal rank, since it seemed odd that the "Mother of all churches" should not have this honor. However, the political power of the four great cities of the empire counted most in the ecclesiastical-political picture that mirrored the empire. The rivalries between the patriarchates accounted for much of the tragic splitting off of Eastern Christendom in the Christological controversies of the 5th century.

At the top of the Christian church in the empire, though not really its head, stood the Christian emperor, the church's protector, supervisor, and the arbiter of its disputes. He summoned and presided over the ecumenical councils which were called to decide matters of universal Christian concern. He confirmed the episcopal elections, though—except for the elections of the bishop of his own city, the patriarch of Constantinople—he usually did not interfere in them. Nevertheless, he exiled bishops deposed by councils, exercised a heavy hand in the proceedings of the councils, and enforced their decisions.

In view of this growth of authorities transcending the jurisdiction of the local bishop, it is interesting to note that in the mid-3rd century Cyprian, the prestigious metropolitan of Carthage in Africa, still maintained that every bishop is ultimately responsible to God alone for his actions as a bishop, for every bishop is an equal successor of the apostles, among whom no one exercised authority over another. This did not mean that he did not consult his colleagues, but that there is an essential equality or parity among them. They are peers.

This was written by Cyprian when he was defending his practice of rebaptizing heretics and schismatics who had received their baptism outside the Catholic Church and now wanted to join it. Rebaptism was a common practice at his time in Africa, but it was angrily denounced by Rome. To back up Rome's argument against the Africans, the bishop of Rome, Stephen, quoted Matthew 16:19 to prove that Peter was given primacy among the apostles. Since the Roman bishop was considered the successor of this apostle, he should therefore be obeyed. Actually prior to this controversy Cyprian himself had written that the unity of the Christian church required that everyone should agree with the bishop of Rome, who as the successor of Peter served as a guarantor of Christian unity. The new situation, however, forced Cyprian to rewrite his tract, "On the Unity of the Catholic Church," in order to defend his episcopal autonomy vis-a-vis Rome. When the Lord gave the Keys to Peter, he now explained, He gave him no other authority than that which He soon after gave to all the other apostles (Matt. 18:18). As a matter of fact, he explained that every bishop is in reality a successor of Peter, who is a symbol of the episcopate. Soon afterwards both Stephen and Cyprian died and the question was left unsettled. Stephen's immediate successors did not press their Petrine authority. It was only from the late 4th century on that the bishops of Rome started to use the Petrine primacy systematically to build up a claim to universal authority on their part. They alone were the spokesmen of Peter.

ROME

The see of Rome had the multiple advantage of being the ancient capital of the Roman Empire and of having the two great apostles Peter and Paul associated with its beginnings. While early Christians spoke of the "double apostolic foundation" of the Roman Christian community, the period under our survey stressed the Petrine origin of the Roman see. Peter was considered the first bishop of Rome, and when the Roman bishops needed to back up their authority vis-a-vis the more remote bishops who did not belong to their jurisdiction as metropolitans, the Petrine foundation was more helpful than an appeal to both Peter and Paul. Since, as they believed, Jesus assigned primacy to Peter among the apostles, and since the apostles certainly appointed successors to carry on their responsibilities, the bishops who hold Peter's chair in Rome inherited his primacy and authority, of which the Keys (Matt. 16:19) were the symbol. It is interesting that no one before the mid-3rd century seemed to have invoked this text to argue for the Roman bishop's preeminence. However, while the Roman see had carried an enormous moral prestige among the early Christians, it had not claimed universal jurisdiction.

Rome was the most important city in the world, and its Christian community was unique in having a double apostolic connection, though surely Jerusalem could have claimed far more on apostolic grounds. Its congregation was certainly the most numerous. It could boast the greatest number of martyrs; it came to have a renown for steadiness in the faith.

STRUCTURE, LEADERSHIP, AND SERVICE

Rome remained orthodox through most of the theological struggles which shook the church, especially the East, during the 4th and 5th centuries. Finally, the church in Rome produced a series of remarkable ecclesiastical statesmen. Its primacy in Christendom was universally recognized. What the other metropolitans, especially African and Eastern bishops, questioned was Rome's universal jurisdiction: the new claim by Roman popes to a legal and not just moral universal authority. (The word "pope" was derived from *papa*, an affectionate and respectful term for father, in church usage by no means limited only to the bishops of Rome.) To the Eastern patriarchs he was a superior only within his own patriarchate, Western Christendom. Among the patriarchs he was considered the first among equals *(primus inter pares)*. This is still the view of the great churches of the East, which to this day do not have the unified and centralized organization which slowly emerged in the West.

Whatever the merits of the papal interpretation of Matthew 16:19, the church was badly shattered by the great theological controversies of the 4th and 5th centuries. To insure its unity, it needed an instrument better than the ecumenical councils which did not succeed in their attempt. Papal leadership in the West gave Western Christendom a unity which the East lacked. Of course, there were no such large and ancient sees in the West to compete with Rome as there were in the East. Also, Latin Europe lacked the theological subtlety to develop so many competing theologies, as did Alexandria and Antioch, among others. The Romans were practical-minded and were absorbed by the problem of law and order. Greek culture, on the other hand, fostered an intellectual curiosity which was not so easily controlled. Thus there was more than one reason for the relative unity of the church in Latin Europe. All the while, Latin-speaking Africa, as we shall see later, seethed with dissension. The problem of Latin Africa's relationship to Rome was settled by the Vandals' complete devastation of North Africa in the early 5th century.

Perhaps the greatest advantage Rome had was the geographical distance of the emperor when he moved to Constantinople, especially when the barbarians inundated the West and submerged the imperial power there. Since the emperor considered himself responsible for the right teaching and unity of the church, the bishops of the East, especially the patriarch of Constantinople, could not move as freely as the Roman bishop. The latter had no one to look continually over his shoulder, whether a nearby patriarch or an emperor.

Among the Roman bishops were several who were not only skillful statesmen and administrators but also great pastors of their own immediate flock and of other church leaders. The greatest of them were popes Leo and Gregory, of the 5th and 6th centuries respectively. They earned for the papacy much of the esteem it came to have by their work as pastors. Gregory the Great (ca. A. D. 600) had a most appealing philosophy of his office and of the pastoral office in general. He coined the term "servant of the servants of God" for the pope as the successor of Peter. He made it clear by action and word that, following the example of their Lord, the apostles and their successors were here to serve, not be served. The bishop's rule, including that of the Roman bishop, was not a form of lordship but of stewardship and service. It rested on the leader's responsibility for his people and always involved respect for the person who was being ruled or admonished. The pope, as any bishop, was to rule primarily by moral authority. Persuasion and example, rather than an appeal to legal subordination, were the proper means of his rule. This did not mean that Gregory hesitated to remove an irresponsible person from his ecclesiastical office. Gregory is sometimes called the "father of medieval papacy," but many of his successors ruled in a different spirit.

PHYSICIANS OF THE SOUL

Gregory the Great wrote an intriguing book on the work and problems of the pastor as a physician of souls. His

Pastoral Rule was given to every medieval Western bishop at his consecration to guide him in pastoral care. The modern reader is struck by its psychological sensitivity and insight. Its author built on the rich pastoral experience of generations of spiritual physicians before him. These were not only bishops and presbyters but also monks who acted as spiritual guides and counselors. Significantly, almost the entire energy of the good pastor, according to Gregory's *Rule*, was spent on the sins of his flock. This preoccupation with sin was perhaps caused by the tradition of spiritual counselors functioning as guides in private repentance, as well as by the influence of monasticism and of St. Augustine on Gregory. Both were introspective in their piety. The introspective tendency and the preoccupation with sin was something new in the history of Christianity and, rather unfortunately, very influential in the development of the religion and psychology of Western man. Its ultimate result can be seen in the case of the guilt-ridden young Luther, the constant self-analysis of the Puritans, and the flourishing of psychiatry in our society. It is noteworthy that such preoccupation with sin is foreign to Eastern Christianity.

Following a long tradition, Gregory sees the pastor as a spiritual *physician* dealing with patients whose diseases he has to discern, diagnose, and treat with appropriate spiritual medicine or surgery. Since not only diseases but also patients differ, the physician—the pastor—has to understand the nature of the disease, whether weakness or sin, as well as the nature of man and each person he wishes to heal. The same treatment cannot be applied to different diseases. Even the same illness in two different personalities has to be treated with different medicine.

Hardened and insensitive sinners need severe rebuke, while others need gentle coaxing or an indirect approach. The arrogant and the hardened usually need to be treated with outer disdain, this disdain being only a means of waking them up; it is never actually to be felt in the heart of the pastor. But sometimes only loving admonition will affect their heart. The timid are to be reprimanded incidentally and indirectly, and this only after some encouragement on some other point. The choleric, while in the state of frenzy, are not to be argued with; if they must be restrained they are to be treated "sparingly, with a certain respectful forbearance."[3] When dealing with someone who is torn by two conflicting evils, the remedy applied to him should be such as to heal both diseases at once. Yet since this is not always a possibility, the spiritual physician has to assess which malady is the more immediately dangerous, and hope that when this cancerous growth is removed occasion will arise when the other ailment can be attended to.

Since we live in a world where the alternatives are not always between black and white but between different shades of grey, a Christian leader must learn to choose between the evils with which he is presented. He is to have a certain recklessness and courage about the evil with which he is left. Thus when counseling a man who is trapped by gluttony and is inclined to show off with his achievements, the pastor can afford to gamble. If gluttony at present seems the more frightening form of demonic possession, he is to encourage him to work at self-control, even if this may increase his love of personal glory. (Gluttony, it should be noted, was a problem which plagued late Roman and medieval society, somewhat like alcoholism and drug addiction plague ours today.) The counselor must not only care about the men he serves; he must also be a shrewd knower of men. This point comes through again and again in Gregory's work.

A good pastor must be well-acquainted with the nature and intricacies of sin, but to Gregory he is not just a psychologist. He must also know something about the work of grace in man, "the mysterious power of God, which comes to us by the Holy Spirit" and which frees men from enslavement to sin. Otherwise the pastor who witnesses so much human weakness and temptation would despair or become callous or trapped himself. Without this grace of God he could easily be repelled by the disclosures or tempted by the temptations he hears described. This Gregory knew from experience. The only remedy against such disgust with one's brothers is to look at one's self and stand in fear, Gregory advises. As far as the temptations are concerned, he brings up an intriguing analogy from the Old Testament. In front of the doors of the ancient temple were lavers (basins) in which worshipers would wash their hands before entering the temple. Naturally, the water would become dirty in the process. "It happens frequently that, while the ruler's [pastor's] mind learns of the trial of others, he also is assailed by the temptations which he gives ear to; for in the case of the laver, too, . . . it is certainly defiled. . . . But the pastor need not fear these things at all, for when God weighs all things exactly, the pastor is the more easily delivered from temptation as he is the more compassionately afflicted by the temptations of others" (*The Rule*, II:5). Here we see that in Gregory's view the good physician of the soul was not a detached analyst. Gregory and his pastors could bear the weight of their job only because they believed that they and their patients were borne up by the compassionate and strong hands of God.

CHRISTIAN OUTREACH

One of the most important results of Gregory's understanding of human nature was its effect on Christian missions to barbarian nations. Gregory the Great launched and directed by correspondence the mission to the English, who had recently settled in and taken over the greater part of Celtic-speaking Britain. The old Britons, largely Christian, had been pushed by them into the Welsh mountains. Gregory selected his former fellow monks, headed by a certain Augustine, to bring the Gospel to the new nation, starting with Canterbury in the south of England. The Irish Christian mission was in the meantime pushing into northern England from Scotland. Augustine was not a particularly clever man, and he referred all the problems he encountered with the heathen culture to Pope Gregory. Gregory instructed him not to try to destroy all the heathen customs, but rather to adopt and only slowly transform what is dear and traditional to the people. So, for instance, the pagan shrines were not to be desecrated but consecrated to Christ and His saints. Old marriage customs were not to be changed before the people had sufficient understanding. The medicine of God's Word was to be administered according to the condition of the patient, so that it might heal and not destroy, be cherished and not hated.

This appreciation of people's sensitivities and cultural differences made the Christian mission in Gregory's time a genuine success. His philosophy was not original. We have seen, for example, how the 4th century adapted the pagan midwinter festivals for Christian use. His philosophy was carried on in Roman Catholic missions, even in the Christian outreach of much later times, as in the work of the Spanish padres with the Indians. They preserved as much as possible of the native cultures. If the Christian church in its work with the barbarians at the beginning of the Middle Ages had been less wise and less elastic, we might never have seen a Christian Europe come out of the debris of the western Roman Empire. At best, it would have been a culture deprived of the different folk traditions which mark today's European nations. Many a ghost tale today still reveals its heathen origin.

Notes
1. For the meaning of the word "see," refer to Note 18 at the end of Chapter 2. The bishop's see came to mean also his jurisdiction, that is, his citywide "parish," or diocese.
2. John Chrysostom, *On the Priesthood*, Bk. III, Ch. 9, *A Select Library of the Nicene and Post-Nicene Fathers* [N & PNF], Vol. IX, First Series (New York: The Christian Literature Co., 1889), p. 49.
3. Gregory the Great, *Pastoral Care*, Bk. III, Ch. 16, *Ancient Christian Writers*, Vol. 11, ed. H. Davis (Westminster, Md.: Newman Press, 1955), p. 139.

5.

MONASTICISM, THE NEW LEAVEN

How did monasticism start? Why and when did Christian men and women start withdrawing from civilization and their own parishes to become monks and nuns, or in the case of men, even hermits? What led to the creation of religious orders? In view of the important role the monastic movement has played in the shaping of Christendom, it is essential to understand its history.

The early church was an elite minority, separate and distinguishable from the rest of society. Its standards and values conflicted with the world it considered vain, rotten, and doomed. Early Christians eagerly awaited a speedy end of the present age and its replacement by the glorious age in the world to come. The hostility and persecutions they met confirmed them in their separateness from society and kept their ranks disciplined and screened. When the awaited end did not come and Christians were more tolerated, it was inevitable that most of them would come to terms with the world, especially as their ranks swelled and Christianity became popular. Security, comfort, and success in the eyes of the world were less scorned by the church, and a large degree of conformity to society followed. When the masses started to pour into the church in the 4th century as a result of Constantine's conversion and changes in imperial policies toward Christians, it became less easy to distinguish Christians from the common run of people. The changed character of the church called forth a movement of protest in the form of a withdrawal from civilization and parish and of a severe asceticism on the part of many earnest Christians. These were the first Christian hermits and ascetics, men and women, who were repelled by the church's compromise with the world.

The root of monastic withdrawal was an ascetic understanding of the call of Christ, which was seen as a summons to a life of self-control and self-denial. Discipleship in the New Testament was often understood as the denial of self and as the forsaking of security and family that tie men down and keep them from giving their whole selves to the spreading of the Good News of God's coming kingdom. Not all who believed in Christ were expected to become disciples in this sense, but it was thought that the core of Jesus' disciples was a group of men who had forsaken all and given themselves to a life of daring adventure. St. Paul was in some respects an ascetic of this type. He urged others to become untrammeled from the cares of this troubled passing age and to be free for the "work of the Lord." This to him involved a life of celibacy when possible. (1 Cor. 7:9-17; 25-26; 29-32)

Each of the early Christian communities had its own ascetics: men and women who had deliberately remained unmarried or widowed ("virgins" and "widows" were official categories on the rolls of the church), kept a minimum of personal property for themselves and dedicated themselves to a life of prayer and the care of the needy in the community. As long as the rest of the congregation of Christians remained separate from society, and persecutions made witnessing for the faith in prison or in the arena as a martyr still a distinct possibility, the ascetics remained one with their home communities.

However, when Christianity became popular and conformed to the world, the ascetics became estranged from the Christian mainstream. Many of them came to feel that living within the parish necessarily entailed a wholesale compromise with society and was inevitably distracting from a life of devotion, self-denial, and contemplation. Since they saw the transformation of their church as a victory for the demonic forces and, in accordance with tradition, believed that the home of the demons was the desert, the Christian ascetics retreated into the wilderness to fight the powers of evil on their home front. The surrender of all the comforts of civilization and home, voluntary hard physical labor, and manful wrestling with all the temptations which come to a man in his loneliness were considered a new form of martyrdom, a witness to and a union with the Lord's suffering by which he triumphed over the world. With the martyrs gone, the monks were now the "athletes" of God.

The first Christian monk was the Egyptian St. Anthony, who sold his inheritance, gave the money to the poor, and withdrew into the sands of Egypt at the turn of the 4th century. He did return to the city during the Diocletian persecution and again later to lend his support to Athanasius in his fight with the forces of Arianism, which shows that he was not one who wished to escape unpleasant confrontations. But otherwise he was a hermit, the founder of an anchorite monasticism, that is, a life in solitude. The immediate inspiration for Anthony's drastic action was his hearing the lesson about Jesus' encounter with the rich young man (Matt. 19: 16-22): "If you would be perfect, go, sell what you possess, and give to the poor, and you will have treasure in heaven; and come, follow Me." These words moved countless other men to leave everything behind and "follow Jesus" in a life of ascetic abandonment of property and home. Anthony was followed by countless admirers—men who wished his counsel or who desired to imitate him—so that he had to withdraw deeper and deeper into the desert to attain the desired (and dreaded) solitude. He is known for his vivid temptations in the form of lurid visions, though this type of temptation seems typical for and invited by his style of life.

Shortly after the start of the anchorite movement, Pachomius started a community (coenobite) monasticism in Egypt. Coenobite monasticism is a Christian communism, at the opposite pole of the extreme individualism of the anchorites. Here persons subjected themselves to a communal ascetic discipline, with hard labor and self-mortification such as fasting, and very sparse meals undertaken in common under the direction of Pachomius, their leader. Complete solidarity with the community, soldier-like obedience, and suppression of all self-assertion were seen by these earnest Christians as necessary parts of the taking up of one's cross. Here is the origin of monasteries and also of female cloisters, for this type of monastic life was a possibility also for women. The communities were directed by an abbot (from *abba*, the Aramaic affectionate term for "father") or an abbess.

A third type of monasticism appeared in the wilderness of Judea in the 5th century: a compromise between the extremes of the solitary life on the one hand and the completely communal life on the other. The monks here did not live together but close to each other and to their spiritual father. They met for meals and prayers in common but spent much time by themselves. This satisfied the individualist who could not have adjusted well to life in a commune but who was not quite ready for complete solitude and desired spiritual guidance from a desert father known and revered for his wisdom and holiness. The arrangement served as spiritual preparation for many a future hermit.

THE RADICALS

The Egyptian and Syrian deserts were famous for their hermits, who were the greatest heroes of the people. The life apart from the community appeared as the greatest sacrifice and surely meant deep holiness. The wrestlers with the demons of the desert came to take the place of the martyrs of old. Villagers and city dwellers sought out the hermits to receive guidance and counsel in their perplexities. Their hermits' sayings and experiences became famous, passed on from mouth to mouth. Most of the monks were simple, uneducated laymen. Their type of life made them the people's philosophers. Their stories and sayings are sometimes shocking to us by their negation of what seems natural and human, especially in the sphere of food and human sexuality. From early times Christian ascetics were intent to live the life of angels instead of flesh-and-blood mortals, thus anticipating already here and now existence in the age of the resurrection (Matt. 22:30). Their stringent fasts were believed to foster chastity.

Yet, alongside the strange and inhuman rigor there is a strand in their stories which is very understanding, very wise, and very human. The true ascetic saint was extremely approachable and had a fatherly attitude to his spiritual children. He was no stranger to human weakness, and his fierceness toward himself was coupled with compassion rather than with intolerance toward others. Since his struggle with Satan was interior, the monk's gaze went inward: he became very introspective and preoccupied with his sins and temptations. The constant self-analysis of monks, a new phenomenon in the history of Christianity as was said before, made them also analysts and counselors of others. They developed the custom of confessing their sins and temptations to their spiritual fathers and became popular confessors themselves.

The early monks were radicals. Their self-mortification, especially of the anchorites who devised their own ascetic exercises, were extreme and often bizarre. Some seemed intent on a slow suicide and self-torture, with their long fasts and vigils and other more ingenious self-punishments. Some monks, while seeking to flee the world, only succeeded in attracting its attention. The famous Simeon Stylites did not live in a desert but on the top of a pillar to get away from impertinent pilgrims who would not leave him alone. Whatever misgivings we might have about this, he considered his action an important witness to detachment from the world, a world which admired him for it. The radical protesters against the church's accommodation to the world were not only an interesting sociological phenomenon; they would have been fascinating objects of psychiatric analysis. Their steeling themselves against all feelings of pleasure and pain made them strikingly similar to the Indian fakirs.

Was there any Indian influence on the monastic movement in the Near and Middle East? The most extravagant feats of asceticism were found in Syria and Mesopotamia.

Anyone acquainted with the Bible can discern non-Christian elements in the attitudes of the ascetics toward the body and the bodily functions and joys. The Biblical understanding of creation involves a great appreciation of the physical aspects of existence. Jesus was criticized for liking to eat and drink in contrast to the ascetic John the Baptist. He was even called "a glutton and a drunkard" (Matt. 11:19). Jesus did not stress the importance of self-control and the danger of passions. The emphasis on restraint and self-control and on the presumed superiority of mind over body was, however, characteristic of philosophies popular in the Greek-influenced world. While there were different philosophical parties, most men lived by a synthesis of elements from the various philosophies, and these all worked to foster an ascetic attitude in life.

Platonic philosophy bequeathed its emphasis on the superiority of the spiritual realm over the "misleading" world of senses. Socrates taught that the body was a prison house of the soul. The Cynics, of whom the most famous was Diogenes who lived naked in a barrel, taught that men should be free from all the cares of the world, especially from the conventions of society, and should develop an utter self-sufficiency by divesting themselves of all that was not absolutely necessary in life. The Epicureans preached the pure pleasures of the spirit. The Stoics emphasized the importance of rational self-control, frugality, and moderation, pointing out the harmful nature of passion and desire. Stoic philosophy and its way of life intended to enable a man to take all privations and losses in his stride. The ascetic discipline was to enable man to be unaffected by what he has or does not have.

All this shows that Christian ascetics were really philosophers more than saints, or rather that they held to a Greek-philosophical interpretation of holiness without knowing it. Philosophical ideas and ideals had so penetrated the spiritual climate of the late-Roman Empire that one simply took them for granted. In this way they became part and parcel of Christianity.

The extremes of Christian asceticism, however, cannot be attributed directly to the influence of Greek philosophy, which extolled moderation as the golden mean. Was the extremism then a result of the intense temperament of the people, or was there an Indian influence? Both probably played a role, though documentation is difficult. However, Mani, a Mesopotamian religious reformer who founded the popular Manichean movement, acknowledged his debt to Buddha, among others, which clearly shows that Mesopotamia was not immune to Indian thought. The areas where Christianity became popular absorbed and cultivated a host of Eastern or Eastern-influenced philosophical and religious ideas and practices. All of them, like Gnosticism and Manicheanism, pitched the spiritual against the physical and cultivated a contempt of the latter. Leaders of the church fought both Gnosticism and Manicheanism and the extremes of asceticism. Nevertheless, the suspicion and low view of the body made their way undetected into Christian mentality. Nobody seemed to notice that this was a subtle infiltration of foreign elements into Christian asceticism and into the mainstream of Christianity. To this day much of Christianity remains affected by it.

While it was the East that gave birth to monasticism and witnessed the flowering of some of its bizarre forms, the West developed its own monastic heroes and "fakirs." The most famous of the Western ascetic radicals was St. Jerome, considered one of the four great fathers of the Western church, the other three being Sts. Ambrose, Augustine, and Gregory. Jerome was born in Italy in the mid-4th century and received a superior education in Latin classical literature. He loved his classics and could not part with them when he settled as a monk in Palestine's Bethlehem. He brought his entire library into his cave, a "luxury" and a comfort over which he never had an easy conscience. He wrote:

> It was many years ago when, for the sake of the kingdom of heaven, I had cut myself off from home, my parents, my sister, my kinsmen and—what was even more difficult—from an accustomed habit of good living. I was going to Jerusalem to be a soldier of Christ. But I could not do without a library which I had collected for myself at Rome by great care and effort. And so, poor wretch that I was, I used to fast and then read Cicero![1]

He was a prodigious writer, not original in his thoughts but masterful in his style. He is famous for the revision of the Latin Bible, the Latin Biblical commentaries, and his witty and biting letters. He undertook the revision of the Latin Bible at the initiative of Pope Damasus because the old Latin translation was not reliable. Its Old Testament was not based on the original Hebrew but on the old Greek version called the Septuagint. Jerome's presence in the East, where he became acquainted with Hebrew and Greek manuscripts and with Eastern (Jewish and Christian) Biblical scholarship, enabled him to arrive at a good knowledge and understanding of the best available Hebrew and Greek manuscripts and thus to produce a more accurate translation of the Bible for Latin-speaking Christians. He was also able to put together valuable Biblical commentaries for them. Biblical and theological scholarship was not as developed in the West as it was in the more cultured and more Christianized East.

The Bible Jerome produced is known as the Vulgate, because it was written in "vulgar" Latin, that is, in the common language of the people *(vulgus)*. Its style was non-classical, just as most of the New Testament had been written in a very common, low-brow Greek. The Vulgate gradually became the standard and only authoritative Bible of the West. Even Luther normally read and quoted from the Bible in this version, although he had mastered Greek and

Hebrew and produced his own German translation from these languages. Until very recently all Roman Catholic translations of the Bible into modern languages had to be based on the Vulgate. Even though modern scholars base their work primarily on Greek and Hebrew Biblical manuscripts, the Vulgate is still a valuable source for them. The reason is that Jerome had at his disposal some important older manuscripts which are no longer available.

When Jerome to his great surprise found that the Hebrew Old Testament did not contain all the books to which Christians were accustomed from their Greek and Latin versions of the Old Testament, he nicknamed these books "Apocrypha," that is, "hidden" or "puzzling" in their origin. He included them in his translation, since they were used in the church's worship. These Apocryphal books form the difference between Catholic and Protestant canons of Scripture. The Protestant Reformers recognized only the "original sources," that is, only the Hebrew text of the Old Testament and the Greek text of the New, as having binding authority.

Jerome was a devotee not only of literature and scholarship but also of the stringent ascetic life, especially of celibacy. Monasticism had not yet taken root in the West and Jerome did everything in his power to foster it, or at least to cultivate asceticism within families. He used for this his powerful pen. Jerome carried on a voluminous correspondence with men and women in the West. His letters to ladies of high rank in Rome, among whom he had many admirers and friends, encouraged them to scorn and forsake the pleasures of family and social life, to become nuns in Palestine if possible, and to train their daughters as ascetics. He pointed out with vivid sarcasm the annoyances of married life, in which he could see nothing but a pointless burden and from which he would have liked to save his lady friends and their innocent daughters. Marriage had only one positive role, as far as he could see: to produce virgins.

The letters make for fascinating and often hilarious

reading. However, his asceticism was not primarily based on a contempt of marriage—he simply was a satirist and his remarks about marriage have to be read with this part of his personality in mind—but on a *mystical* view of voluntary Christian virginity. The Christian virgin was married to Christ, and how could any earthly union compete with that? The concept of a mystical marriage between God or Christ and His people is of course Biblical. In the Bible, however, it is the *community* which is "betrothed" to God or His Christ. Christian mysticism, beginning with Origen in the early 3rd century, applied the analogy also to the union of the individual soul with God. This became a very strong element in Christian asceticism, where it came to be assumed that the heavenly union replaces the earthly instead of existing alongside it. The elevated status of female Christian martyrs and of virgin women (as well as women's scholarly potentialities, in Jerome's view) gave the woman a new, high status in Christianity. She did not exist just for the sake of man nor was she dependent on him. She was not necessarily the "weaker sex." It is needless to say how damaging these ascetic views were for the status of marriage, no matter how much the church stressed that marriage was a creation of God sanctified by Christ.

Jerome was highly respected and admired by many people in the West, for they were so proud of having at last one great Western ascetic, brilliant writer, and erudite scholar. He was therefore very influential in spreading monastic ideas in Rome, although its bishops were conservative, given to common sense, and therefore suspicious of this new and extravagant movement flourishing in the East. Yet it was Gaul which produced the first Western monks. The hero of Gaul was St. Martin, a soldier who tore his winter mantle in two to cover a shivering beggar and then in a dream learned that he had really clothed Christ in this poor brother. Martin founded a monastic community and also fostered monasticism when he later became the bishop of Tours. The asceticism of early Gallic monasticism was severe. It was influenced by Eastern radicals and itself became the inspirer of the all-important Celtic (Gaelic) monasticism of the Irish.

REFORMERS AND PIONEERS IN CHRISTIAN OUTREACH

The excesses of asceticism and the extreme individualism of the anchorite monastic movement east of Egypt (Pachomius' community monasticism did not spread there) did not stay uncriticized even among men favoring monasticism. (St.) Basil of Caesarea (330-79), considered one of the four "Great Fathers of the Eastern church" along with Sts. Athanasius, Gregory of Nazianzus "the Theologian," and John of Antioch (Chrysostom), was taken by the ascetic ideal but thought that it was distorted by the monks' competing with one another in their ascetic feats. These seemed to be pursued only as ends in themselves and to scorn the good gifts of God. He believed such monks were concentrating on themselves instead of on God and the neighbor, the proper objects of the Christian's concern. Yet he agreed with the ascetic ideal of virginity as a means of self-control. He could regard a disciplined life in withdrawal from the hustle of society as an aid to contemplation. He did not disdain nature.

Basil was a gifted and highly educated man, with a talent for organization. He organized a monastic community in the midst of a beautiful woody and mountainous area of Pontus, near his native Cappadocia (in today's Turkey), and drew up organizational rules for his type of community. In a way he picked up where Pachomius had left off, since his ideal was to establish a Christian community whose life together would renew in the church the spirit of the early Christian community. The ascetic life which Basil envisioned was disciplined, but moderate and humane; it was to foster the study of Scripture and theology, the praise and contemplation of God, and the service of the brother. A monk in his community was not allowed to pursue any ascetic extravagances. Basil's monastic *Rules* (manuals) prescribed the pattern of the monk's life as a communal life that left ample time for individual study and contemplation.

The monks had to submit to the direction of their superior or else leave. There was no place for spiritual virtuosos in his community. Basil stressed the importance of a wholesome, modest diet and of sufficient sleep. A monk was to be fit for work. Deeply steeped in the Greek culture, Basil believed in moderation. As Basil saw it, the ascetic life freed the monk so that he might concern himself with his brother. The monks were to open themselves to one another and lived a life of mutual dialog. The monastic community was to embody Christian service and love. It had a deeply social purpose.

To insure stability for the monastic community, Basil introduced the novitiate, or a period of probation, and lifelong vows of poverty, chastity (celibacy), and obedience. Life in the monastery, according to Basil's rules, had a regular rhythm consisting of manual, mainly agricultural, labor, study, fixed hours of community psalm singing and prayers, common meals, the sharing of one's thoughts and problems with one's brothers (Basil made confession and spiritual guidance a regular feature of monastic life), private meditation, and rest. The monastery was ruled by a superior and a council of the better-educated monks. Later, when Basil as bishop established monasteries in cities, social work took the place of manual labor for the city monks.

In his essays on the ascetic life, Basil stressed the freedom which detachment from worldly cares and ambitions brings. The monk is like a soldier: totally at the disposal of his heavenly Commander; he is not tied to property, place, or family; he is outwardly and inwardly free to devote himself to the service of God. This did not mean to Basil that married people were detached from God, or that monks stood above the church and did not need it. This is what some ascetics thought. Basil's monasticism was linked with the life of the wider Christian community. He himself left his retreat to serve the church in a world that needed men of such a free and devoted spirit. He became one of the great bishops of history, a pioneer in the establishment of social welfare institutions, and the leader of the Nicene forces in the struggles of the later 4th century.

The monks reacted against a worldly church, wanting to return to the life of the early Christians. Basil shared their desire, but he saw that the monastic community was not a substitute for the larger church. The latter had an assignment in the world of its time and could not return to the first century, when the church was a tiny minority. The larger church, however, needed the witness of the monastic community, which embedded the ideals of early Christianity, in order to receive a better perspective on its life in secular society. Basil's *Rules* set the pattern for the future development of both Eastern Orthodox and Latin monasticism. His conception of the relationship of the ascetic movement to the wider church became a reality in the history of Christianity, with monasticism serving as a "city set on a hill" and a "light set high" for the struggling church. Whenever the church compromised with the world, ascetic life brought forth reform in the church. Even Luther was a monk, and he did not discard the monk's cowl as soon as he became a reformer. Monastic life and religious orders often went astray or became static, but amazingly there always appeared reformers who recalled them to a new understanding of their role.

Celtic (Irish) monasticism served as such a reforming, civilizing, and evangelizing element in barbarian Western Europe. The Irish church from the days of St. Patrick in the 5th century was permeated by the ascetic ideal. Patrick, who as a young boy was kidnapped from his native Britain and was sold into slavery in Ireland, after some years managed to escape to Gaul, where he became a monk and bishop. He returned to Ireland, which he and his monks converted to the Christian faith and the monastic ideal. Celtic monasticism was severe. It advocated especially the ancient Christian ascetic sacrifice of one's own homeland in voluntary self-exile into faraway places. That is also how, in imitation of the homeless Christ with His disciples, the Irish St. Columba with his 12 monks settled in the 6th century on the far-off Scottish Isle of Iona, from which Christianity penetrated Scotland and northern England. The ideal of voluntary exile explains why so many Irish monks were found in early-medieval France and Germany. That was their "wilderness," their parallel of the desert.

It was in response to the undisciplined life of the still half-pagan Franks that the private confession and penitential discipline in use by monks was introduced by the Irish into the life of the ordinary Christians whom they served as spiritual guides. The Irish developed very influential penitential guidelines for the use of confessors, the "friends of the soul," to enable them to determine the appropriate penance for different offenders. So when a man had committed violence, for example, he was to move around unarmed as his form of penance. This was one of the hardest things to do in the rough-and-ready society of the day.

The Irish exiles' zeal and work, bringing a renewal of Christian life and ministry to the Frankish church, deeply influenced much of Western Christendom. In the Irish monasteries classical culture was preserved for the West, for their monks came to cultivate and spread the Latin tongue and literature that had been almost lost in barbarian Europe.

To St. Benedict of Nursia, Italy, in the 6th century fell the lot of bringing to Western monasticism moderation, stability, regularity, and a deeply ingrained community spirit. He was a student of the works of the Eastern monk Cassian,[2] who introduced a moderate and mystically inclined community monasticism into southern Gaul in the early 5th century. Monasticism in the West had tended to be what it had been east of Egypt prior to Basil's reform: erratic, individualistic, and extreme in its asceticism. Benedict's monks had to vow the "conversion of their way of life," obedience to their superiors, and stability of residence. Benedict agreed with church authorities that the wandering monk was too much of a free-lancer, often irresponsible, idle, disturbing, and hard to control. He was a vagabond. Benedict was not thinking so much of the Celtic communities in exile as of the individualistic ascetics who moved from monastery to monastery, never to settle down. Benedict thought that a monk needed the discipline of staying with his monastic community and being under the supervision of his abbot.

Benedict not only founded his famous monastery at Monte Cassino, which set the pattern for the entire future of monasticism in the West (Benedictine monasticism ultimately replaced the Celtic type), but he also composed the classic Benedictine *Rule* that became its charter. Like Basil's *Rules*, it stressed the importance of obedience in the monastery, though there was a remarkably democratic element in the monastery's form of government. The basic motto of Benedictine monasticism was *ora et labora*, "pray and work." Benedict believed that idleness provided too much of an opportunity for the devil, and so he curbed leisure and even shortened prayers. "Let prayer be short and pure," said his *Rule*. The monk was to be almost always occupied with something constructive, lest his mind become prey to temptations, as was the case in the hermits' prolonged contemplations and prayers. In view of the Roman Empire's lack of appreciation of the inherent value and dignity of manual labor, the cultivation of such labor in monasteries was of profound significance for the attitude toward work in Christian civilization; it was no longer just something fit for slaves. There is an interesting link between the monks' labor and the ancient Jewish tradition that every rabbi had to earn his living by the work of his hands.

Monks were not allowed to keep any private possessions. They were pioneers in agricultural methods in the underdeveloped barbarian lands where they staked out their monasteries. They cultivated fine crafts and excelled in artistic handcopying and illuminating (illustrating by means of miniatures) of books. The Irish especially were early masters in this art. The Benedictines followed in their footsteps, also in preserving and spreading the cultural and churchly heritage of antiquity in the young nations of western and central Europe. The Eastern monks did this for the emerging new nations in Eastern Christendom. Through the monasteries both the writings of the ancient church and the pagan classics were passed on to the civilization which was to emerge from the ruins of the Western Roman Empire. The Benedictine monks, like the Irish and eventually also Eastern monks, were also important missionaries among the heathen and half-heathen barbarian nations, whether they went to them with the express purpose of converting them to Christianity, as was the case with the mission to England, or whether they simply settled in an area and influenced their surroundings.

As in Basil's *Rules,* the Benedictine Rule divided the monk's day into time for work, for the study of Scripture and meditation, for a common meal, and for the regular brief "Hours" of community psalm singing and prayers. The seven divine offices, or services, were: Matins-Lauds and Prime in the early hours of the morning; the Terce, Sext, and None during the hours of work; Vespers after work; and Compline to complete the day. The *Rule* provided for the daily reading of Cassian's *Conferences* in the community's assemblies. Cassian's writings mediated to the West the experience of the Egyptian desert and a systematic science of the spiritual life as it was developed by an Eastern mystic and monastic reformer, Evagrius. It was Evagrius who invented the concept of principal, or "root," sins. He regarded eight root sins as the basis of all others. (Gregory the Great took the list as the basis of his list of the seven "capital sins," which he saw as rooted in the two principal sins of false pride and lust: vainglory, envy, anger, dejection [despair], avarice, gluttony, and the love of luxury. The list became an important teaching tool all through the Middle Ages.) Evagrius also established the classical stepping stones of contemplation, beginning with a contemplation of the visible world, then rising to the invisible, and climaxing with the mystery of God. The highest level of prayer, he taught, was a wordless state in which the worshiper is wrapped up in the contemplation of God.

In the troubled times and upheavals of an age that saw a new world being born, Benedictine monasteries were veritable havens of peace, civilization, and stability. They attracted many by the quiet, humane, purposeful, and noble life they offered. Monasticism provided also an important role for women, for in monastic communities women were autonomous and could develop their initiative and potential for learning and leadership. In several cases women became founders and heads (abbesses) of double monasteries, for men and women. Female religious communities compensated in part for the rather unfortunate absence of the deaconess and "widow" from the church's parish ministry at the end of the Middle Ages. The monastic movement may actually have caused the disappearance of the services of deaconesses and "widows," because it swept the congregation's ascetics away into the retreat of hermitages and monasteries.

It is difficult to stress enough the importance of the monastic movement for Christendom. Its asceticism may have had a harmful effect on the understanding of the true Christian life, interpreting it as a life removed from an active involvement in the "world" and "rising above" the natural joys and instincts, especially those of the sexual relationship, as if they were not good gifts of God. Nevertheless, once Christianity had become the religion of the majority, and the Christian way of life had lost its original and distinctive character, the church needed a separate corps of men and women who would give up the values and ambitions of society, bear witness to the challenge of the Gospel to leave everything and follow Christ, keep the centrality and art of prayer and meditation before the eyes of Christians, and stand out as an example of the solidarity which marks the true Christian community. Though monasticism was not originally intended to serve the church and the world (as we might understand the following of Christ to involve), it did become a valuable agency for the service of Christ in the world, transforming the world it scorned and renewing the church life it fled. It functioned as salt and leaven in the dough of Christendom.

Notes

1. From Jerome's Letter 22, 30.1, as transl. by C. C. Mierow in *Letters of St. Jerome*, Vol. I, *Ancient Christian Writers*, Vol. 33 (1963), pp. 165-6.
2. For Cassian see also Appendix, p. 162.

6.

ST. AUGUSTINE, THE GREAT TEACHER OF THE WEST

The truly great original thinkers of the church in the first centuries were all Easterners. The only partial exception was the North African Tertullian at the turn of the 3rd century, the father of Latin theology. Yet the last towering ancient theologian was a Westerner, again a North African, Aurelius Augustine, bishop of Hippo in today's Algeria. He was born in the mid-4th century, the century of the development of a Roman Christian culture. He died in 430 during the Vandal siege of Hippo. It was the end of an era: the time of the collapse of Roman rule over the West. Augustine was a brilliant heir of the harvest of his era, the harvest of a rich classical and Christian culture. He was a dynamic and creative thinker and writer, and his influence is stamped on the thought of Western Christendom to the present. Both Roman Catholicism and Protestantism are at their deepest level Augustinian.

Although his mother Monica attempted to rear Augustine as a Christian, he spurned the church and the Bible as a young man because he thought that Christianity was just for the simple. It was only after a tortuous intellectual and moral quest — he was a Manichean for 9 or 10 years and then he became a deep skeptic — that he became a Christian and embraced Baptism in his early 30s. He was deeply steeped in the Latin classics and was a professor of rhetoric, a study which was essential to a law or civil service career.

On the basis of his remorseful *Confessions*, written many years after, he is generally considered to have led a wild youth. This judgment is however grossly exaggerating the matter. He went through his adolescent problems, but at the age of 17 he settled down to living with a woman whom he deeply loved and to whom he remained faithful for the next 14 years until his mother broke up their household and arranged for a socially advantageous marriage. Imperial and social laws made marriage of middle-class citizens with people of lower rank an impossibility. So society and the church considered common-law marriages acceptable and moral as long as faithfulness was maintained. This certainly was Augustine's case. He had not been a profligate. His stern judgment on his sexual past was certainly due to the influence of Manicheanism and of Platonic philosophy, neither of which had any appreciation of man's psychosomatic nature. Both considered the sexual impulse a bar to attaining a truly spiritual or philosophical existence.

While teaching in Milan, Augustine was much impressed by its bishop, Ambrose. Ambrose's sermons aroused Augustine's interest by their oratorical skill, intelligence, philosophical orientation, and their resort to an allegorical interpretation of the Old Testament wherever given passages seemed offensive or irrelevant. In Ambrose and his Neoplatonic circle Augustine at last found a Christianity worthy of his intellectual respect. Augustine was converted both to Neoplatonic philosophy and to Christianity. He saw little difference between them at the time. Under this influence Augustine decided to embrace a philosophical-Christian life in ascetic retreat from society. He was baptized and returned to his native town in Africa, forming a semimonastic philosophical community around him in which he hoped to spend the rest of his life in contemplation. Contrary to all his plans and wishes, he was forced to become presbyter in the nearby city of Hippo. Five years later he became bishop of Hippo. His ecclesiastical responsibilities involved him in the life and thought of the church, especially in the thought of the Bible, and made him a theologian. He became a prodigious writer and campaigner in all the theological and ecclesiastical issues of the day and soon became the intellectual leader not only of Roman Africa but of the entire Latin-speaking Christendom.

Apart from his numerous expositions of Scripture and his huge work, *On the Trinity*, which stressed the oneness of the triune God, Augustine's writings concentrated for the most part on current controversies. His earliest writings as a Christian show how deeply affected he was by Neoplatonic philosophy. The most important of his early works are his anti-Manichean writings. In them he takes issue with the Manichean contention that evil is an eternal principle, that evil is a being which matches God and is responsible for the creation of luckless mankind imprisoned in the flesh, the flesh being the source of human slavery and tragedy.

It was because Augustine opposed the negative view the Manicheans had of bodily existence that he came to attack the use of contraception, a practice advocated by the sect because it did not want to bring souls into the flesh by the act of procreation. Conception was considered by them a tragedy, for they taught that prior to it the soul of the child existed in the higher spheres untrammeled by the world of matter. Augustine as a Christian affirmed the essential goodness of bodily existence as the creation of a good God, and therefore he condemned contraception. Influenced by Greek philosophy, he saw passion as a sign of disorder in man, attributing it to man's Fall. He did not see passion as inherent in sexuality as God had intended it, but believed procreation to be the only true function of sexual union. His teaching had an enormous effect on Western Christendom's attitude to sexuality. Its originally anti-Manichean setting came to be lost from sight.

Augustine now denied the eternal and independent nature of evil and the claim that the flesh is the source of man's evil. Following Neoplatonic teaching, he argued that evil is simply the absence of good and of God, just as darkness is the absence of light. This solved for him the agonizing problem of the whence and why of evil in the world. Man has simply misused his freedom and turned away from God, the source of goodness and life. Human life is not determined by evil powers beyond man's and God's control. Yet, Augustine said, a man's mind cannot arrive at liberating truth simply by the power of reasoning, as the Manicheans claimed. The church is the teacher of God's revelation to man, and for man to begin to understand God and what the world is all about, he has first to believe the church's creed. This furnishes the key to understanding and enables reason to find light. As Augustine put it, "I believe in order to understand." Since the Manichean sect was the most serious rival of the Christian church at that time, Augustine's polemic was invaluable; it has exercised enormous influence on Christian philosophy and on the Christian understanding of the relationship of faith and reason.

Beginning with his ordination, Augustine was involved in the problem of the Donatist schism. He devoted many writings to the problem and issues raised by it. This split in the Latin-speaking church of North Africa was a consequence of the last persecution of Christians at the beginning of the 4th century. The imperial authorities had demanded the surrender of Christian books. The clergy who complied with the demand, even those who handed in heretical or even medical books just to hand in something, were dubbed *traditores*, that is, "surrenderers." They were regarded as unworthy compromisers by many zealous Christians in the West. In the view of the zealous African Christians, the traitors' action canceled their membership in the church of the martyrs and made their ministerial actions null and void. They could not, by their laying on of hands, pass on the Spirit, since they no longer possessed it themselves. It was believed that they desecrated every sacred action in which they participated.

This conviction led a group of North African Christians, called "Donatists" after their leader Donatus, to separate themselves from the bishops and churches they considered tainted by their surrender to government pressure. Their exaltation of Christian heroism appealed to vast

ST. AUGUSTINE, THE GREAT TEACHER

numbers. They claimed that they alone were the true church and that the Catholic Church no longer had valid ministries and sacraments. Thus the latter could not be a community of salvation.

The result was a split in the African church. Catholic Christians, of course, disclaimed the accusations. The bitter schism lasted for generations. Apart from the scandal of Christians "splitting the seamless robe of Christ" and rending the church in two, there were some profound theological implications in the controversy. To heal the schism, Augustine came to grips with them in his anti-Donatist writings.

The greatest reproach of Augustine against those who separated themselves from their fellow Christians because of their lack of purity was that the purists (the Donatists in this case) lacked charity and abounded in pride, the greatest of all sins. Whatever good they might have done was destroyed by their pride and lack of charity. Even the work of the sacraments was of no lasting effect in those who live in lovelessness, said Augustine, for there is no lasting forgiveness of sin where there is no charity. Moreover, Augustine claimed, the purists were wrong when they thought that the church could be pure before the separation of the "tares from the wheat" at the final harvest. The church in the present world is a "mixed body." Only a part of it, known to God alone, belongs to the "true body" of Christ which, according to Augustine, also contains God's elect who at present are not within the church. Nevertheless, the church with all its faults is an agent of God's kingdom. The necessarily mixed character of the church does not mean that no church discipline is to be exercised, Augustine explained. Let discipline be performed, but with gentleness and with the hands of a careful surgeon.

Since no man can see into the hearts (and sometimes even into the past) of the ministers, the validity of the sacraments cannot be made dependent on their spiritual state. The members of the clergy do not act in the name of their own personal holiness but in the name of God, whose ministers, that is, servants, they are. The sacraments, so long as they are celebrated according to Christ's institution, are means of grace because they belong to Christ and His church, wherever and by whomever they are administered. When a person is ordained to the service of God, he is marked for life as such. The mark, or *character* in Greek and Latin, is indelible, that is, it cannot be wiped out by his sins. God provides this security, so that there might be no uncertainty as to one's baptism. The Donatist position, Augustine showed, could lead all men to despair if everything is made to depend on the holiness of the clergy.

However ludicrous the origins of the Donatist schism may seem to us, the schismatics' insistence on the purity of the church and on the necessity of a Spirit-filled clergy reflected the earlier Christian tradition of the church when it was still a select body, conscious of the presence of the Spirit of God in their midst. Nevertheless, as is clear to any reader of Augustine's argument as we have just sketched it, Augustine had to reach the conclusions he did for the furthering of sanity and charity among the Christians in Africa at that time. Among Western Christians ever since — the Eastern Church did not face the Donatist problem — his insights have been a strong factor. We are so influenced by his teaching that his points seem obvious. We may not even be aware of how pioneering Augustine's thoughts were at that time.

One problem the Donatists created was that the government became involved and attempted to enforce an end to the schism. From the government's point of view, church divisions created social disunity and were therefore harmful to the commonweal. Augustine was at first opposed to any governmental pressure on the Donatists, because he feared social and legal disabilities would bring about only feigned conversions. But when many Donatists became Catholic on hearing Catholic sermons after their own churches were closed and their clergy expelled, Augustine decided that the Donatist error would never have become clear to the people without government pressure to attend

ST. AUGUSTINE, THE GREAT TEACHER

Catholic services. He concluded that this justified the government's intervention. He even found a Gospel verse—the "compel them to come in" text from the parable of the Great Banquet—to give it Scriptural footing. In Augustine's time no tortures or deaths were inflicted on nonconformist schismatics. Unfortunately, Augustine's quotation of the "compel them to come in" verse was used as a theological vindication for inhuman religious persecutions in later medieval Christendom.

The next issue in which Augustine, who was quite obviously a fighter, was involved was the Pelagian controversy. Pelagius was a very morally concerned British monk who was shocked by the moral laxity of Christians in high social circles in Rome at the beginning of the 5th century. He stressed therefore the Christian's moral responsibility versus a take-it-easy reliance on grace or the Manichean pessimism that man was a powerless slave of evil. He taught a vigorous Christian life in accord with the laws of God and the example of Christ. When a man has been shown what is right, there is no reason for his not doing it, he thought. Man has only to be taught right and then make up his mind to follow it.

Pelagius was deeply influenced by Greek philosophical thought that saw no separation between reason and will. To argue that man cannot help but do wrong because mankind has been corrupted by Adam's fall is simply to seek for excuses. Men are certainly affected by Adam's and his descendants' sins because of the bad examples they have continuously before them. But they also have the example of Christ, who did not sin. The Pelagian theologians—and there were some able thinkers among them—thought that to claim that man is simply born sinful and that he has a corrupted nature is a Manichean way of thinking. It does not see man's nature as the workmanship of God and denies man's moral responsibility. For if man is not free to live the life God commands him to live, why should God command it or blame man when he fails? Of course, God by His grace forgives a penitent sinner, but repentance means that a man sets out in earnest to do what God commands.

Augustine was concerned that Pelagius did not appreciate the inner conflict by which a man was torn between what he knew was right and wrong, that he disregarded that man was often powerless to do the right he actually willed. Pelagius did not understand fully the complexity of human nature that Augustine knew so well from his personal experience in his youth and that he also found in St. Paul's reflection on the human predicament (Rom. 7:15). In consequence, Pelagius did not perceive man's desperate need for God's Spirit to provide the power to live according to God's will. Yet this is what God gives to those who believe in Christ (Rom. 8:2). This was how Augustine interpreted Paul's teaching of justification by grace through faith: Believers became just men by the grace of God. The empowering gift of the Spirit was what Augustine understood by "grace." He noted that this was missing in Pelagius.

Augustine argued that man's nature was corrupt and no longer what God had created when He made the first man. Augustine saw mankind in its sin as an organic whole: All men in history are vitiated by the first man's Fall, because they are his descendants. This is how Augustine interpreted "original sin," which he saw as hereditary, as passed on through the reproductive process. This was his way to interpret Paul's words that all have sinned in Adam (Rom. 5:12). In this way he explained the puzzling fact that men have always and everywhere from their childhood tended to evil. Augustine appealed also to the church's practice of infant Baptism, for, he said, if children are not born sinful, why does the church baptize them? (Pelagius simply referred to John 3:5 for an answer: Baptism is not only for the remission of sins, but it is necessary for entering the kingdom of God.) Although human beings are born sinful, they are responsible for their sins because they often even do not wish to do what is right. Besides, there is the corporate guilt of mankind, for it is one entity with Adam. This was Augustine's retort to Pelagius' arguments. Augustine's teaching on the corruption

ST. AUGUSTINE, THE GREAT TEACHER

(depravity) of human nature, on man's powerlessness to pull himself together, and on his total dependence on God's grace became extremely influential on Western theological thinking, especially on the theology of the Lutheran and Calvinist Reformations.

If everything depends on God and His grace, why do some men do right and others not? Does not God will all men to be saved? One answer, of course, was that God did not force His grace on anyone; our volition does not always come from God, as Augustine had said. But eventually the heated debate drove Augustine to a rigid doctrine of a double predestination. God's grace is irresistible, he said; otherwise no man could attain salvation, because of his own fickle will. So God has graciously chosen men on whom He would bestow His irresistible grace, which will enable them to persevere in faith and good works until the end. This has nothing to do with any merits on their part, for grace is gratis. The rest of mankind God has left to its own devices, thus predestining it to eternal perdition, a state that all men have deserved. Augustine appealed to Romans 9—11 for Scriptural support. He interpreted Paul's discussion of the relationship of Jews and Gentiles in God's plan of salvation as if it pertained to the predestination of individuals instead of Jews and Gentiles as such. His interpretation has exercised profound influence over the mind of the West, the double predestination finding its most fervent exponent in John Calvin.

In the East Augustianism made little impression. To the men of Augustine's time this teaching of predestination did not seem as shocking and frustrating as it does to the modern mind. Ancient man was a fatalist. In the Roman Empire it was commonly believed that man's life and its outcome were literally "written in the stars" or were determined by an unjust, irrational, and unmerciful Chance or Fate that ruled even over the gods. Thus in his time, the determinism of Augustine would not strike the non-Christian as absurd. Its effect on Christians was something else again. Christian teaching had stressed the freedom of man versus the ancient fatalism that undermined all sense of moral responsibility and moral will power in life. (Eastern theology has still retained the accent on man's freedom.) Thus Augustine's determinism was shocking to many Christians. But to others it gave a sense of purpose which the unforeseeable accidents in life had seemed to deny. It certainly seemed better to believe in the purposeful and mysterious plan of God, and in the hope which it brought to at least a portion of mankind, than to believe in the capricious game of Chance.

It is fascinating to see that the Augustinian and Muslim doctrine of an immutable divine decree, far from making men passive in life, created a hardy, aggressive, and dynamic race of men, as can be best seen in the early Muslim conquerors and in the Calvinist Puritans who defied the decrees of the king and tamed the American wilderness.

The most famous of Augustine's works are his *Confessions,* the first spiritual autobiography, and his *City of God,* a monumental series of reflections on human social existence and human history. Augustine's *Confessions,* impassionately written in the form of a prolonged prayer examining the underlying motives in his life up to his conversion, is poetry in prose. As to content, it is an introspective self-analysis. As pointed out earlier, its brooding introspection and the preoccupation with the depths of the human psyche blazed, for better and for worse, a new trail in the development of Western culture. The reader may think Augustine has somewhat overdone it when he sits in judgment on his childhood and his youth. Yet Augustine's purpose was not to wade in his former wickedness but to show how restless and perverse the human soul is until it finds its rest in God, and how God's providence guides men unawares.

The writing of the *City of God* was prompted by the fall of "Eternal Rome" into the hand of barbarians in 410 and by the cry of dismay it raised on the part of pagans and Christians alike. When Christians wondered why God had "forsaken" Christian Rome, pagans retorted that the ancient gods had forsaken Rome as a punishment for its defection

ST. AUGUSTINE, THE GREAT TEACHER

to the Christian God. Rome, they said, began to decline as soon as Christians began to multiply and the cult of the gods became neglected. Augustine wrote to give to both bewildered Christians and embittered pagans a better perspective on history and empires. He appealed to the history of previous empires and that of the Roman Empire to show that all history is a story of violence and disasters, conquests and defeats — the fruit of men's fear and self-love. Military victories are not a result of moral and religious merit. The Roman Empire, in spite of the ancient Roman virtues and its present Christian faith, is no exception in the history of nations. It was not the "City of God." The expansion and the peace of the empire had cost much bloodshed and misery. As a Briton had wryly noted, "The Romans make a desert and call it peace."

Rome, as other empires in their times, was a useful instrument of God's providence in history, for its borders did provide some peace, safety, order, and relatively just laws. Yet because of the destruction every empire has sown, it will reap destruction, and Rome, too, deserves it. If in God's judgment its end has come, it is not an ultimate disaster. The empire, of course, has the duty of defending its citizens against the onslaught of the barbarians, but men should see beyond the present struggle. The church will have a task among the conquerors; it is not tied down to the Roman or any other way of life. Moreover, it will find lasting and just peace not within the flux of history but beyond it, in the kingdom of heaven, according to Augustine.

The immediate result of Augustine's argument was to deflate the Roman Empire, which many Christians unconsciously tended to equate with the kingdom of God. Augustine's views helped to make men open to the purposes of God that lay hidden in the uncertain future. Augustine provided the Western church, on the threshold of a new age, with a philosophy of realism, flexibility, and hope with which to face and conquer the new future.

APPENDIX:

READINGS FROM PRIMARY SOURCES

NO. 1 – RELIGION AND EMPIRE

A Certificate of Conformity in A. D. 250

     1st handwriting: To the commission chosen to superintend the sacrifices at the village of Alexander's Isle. From Aurelius Diogenes, son of Satabous, of the village of Alexander's Isle, aged 72 years, with a scar on the right eyebrow. I have always sacrificed to the gods, and now in your presence in accordance with the edict I have made sacrifice . . . and partaken of the sacred victims. . . . 2nd hand: I, Aurelius Syrus, saw you and your son sacrificing. 3rd hand. . . 1st hand: The year one of the Emperor Caesar Gaius . . . Decius. . . . Epiph. 2 [June 26, 250]. (J. R. Knipfing, *Harvard Theological Review*, 16 [Cambridge, Mass.: Harvard U. Press, 1923], p. 363; slightly altered. In J. Stevenson, *A New Eusebius* [London: SPCK, 1965], p. 228.) — For the imperially-enforced **pagan sacrifices and the required certificates see pp. 12-13 in** Chapter 1. (Note: *Page numbers in these cross-references, by which the material in the Appendix is correlated with subjects treated in the chapters, pertain to the pages of this present book.*)

     3. . . . Galerius Maximus [proconsul]: Are you Thascius Cyprianus? Cyprian: I am. G. M.: The most sacred Emperors have commanded you to conform to the Roman rites. C.: I refuse. G. M.: Take heed for yourself. C.: . . . In

so clear a case I may not take heed. 4. Galerius, after briefly conferring with his judicial council, with much reluctance pronounced the following sentence: You have long lived an irreligious life [not worshipping the gods] and have drawn together a number of men bound by an unlawful association, and professed yourself an open enemy to the gods and religion of Rome. The pious, most sacred and august Emperors . . . have endeavored in vain to bring you back to conformity with their religious observances—therefore . . . the authority of the law shall be ratified in your blood. . . . G. M.: It is the sentence of this court that Thascius Cyprianus be executed with the sword. C.: Thanks be to God. (From the *Acta Proconsularia* of St. Cyprian, in J. Stevenson, op. cit., p. 261 f.)

Persecution on the Eve of Victory

IX. X.8. . . . It was enacted by their majesties Diocletian and Maximinian that the meetings of Christians should be abolished. . . . VIII.II.4. March 303. . . . Imperial edicts were published everywhere ordering that the churches be razed to the ground, that the Scriptures be destroyed by fire, that those holding office be deposed and they of the household be deprived of freedom, if they persisted in the profession of Christianity. 5. This was the first edict against us. But not long after other decrees were issued, which enjoined that the rulers of the churches in every place be first imprisoned and thereafter every means be used to compel them to sacrifice. (Eusebius, *Ecclesiastical History* [the first documented history of the church], VIII. ii. 4, in Henry Bettenson, *Documents of the Christian Church* [New York: Oxford U. Press, 1956], p. 21.) April 304. . . . Imperial edicts were issued, in which, by a general decree, it was ordered that all the people without exception should sacrifice in the several cities and offer libations to the idols. (Eusebius, *On the Palestinian Martyrs*, III.1, in Bettenson, p. 21.)—For persecutions see pp. 12-13.

The Conversion of Emperor Constantine in 312

44.5 Constantine was directed in a dream to mark the heavenly sign of God on the shields of his soldiers and thus to join battle. He did as he was ordered and with the cross-shaped letter X, with its top bent over, he marked Christ on the shields [and his army was victorious]. (From Lactantius' *On the Death of the Persecutors,* written before 318, in Stevenson, p. 299.)

I.28. 1 [Constantine] besought his father's god in prayer . . . to help him in his present difficulties. . . . About noon, when the day was already beginning to decline, he saw with his own eyes the trophy of a cross of light in the heavens, above the sun, and an inscription, CONQUER BY THIS attached to it. At this sight he himself was struck with amazement, and his whole army also . . . witnessed the miracle. . . . Then in his sleep the Christ of God appeared to him with the sign which he had seen in the heavens, and commanded him to make a likeness of that sign . . . and to use it as a safeguard in all his engagements with his enemies. (Eusebius, *Life of Constantine,* written ca. 338. Stevenson, pp. 299 f.) — For Constantine's conversion see p. 13.

The Toleration Edict of 313

48.2. When we, Constantine Augustus and Licinius Augustus, had happily met at Milan, and were conferring about all things which concern the advantage and security of the state, we thought that amongst other things which seemed likely to profit men generally, the reverence paid to the Divinity merited our first and chief attention. Our purpose is to grant both to the Christians and to all others full authority to follow whatever worship each man has desired; whereby whatsoever Divinity dwells in heaven may be benevolent and propitious to us, and to all who are placed under our authority. . . . (Lactantius, op. cit., in Stevenson, p. 300.) — Final peace for the church came only in 324, when

Constantine became the sole ruler of the entire Roman Empire.

Sunday Becomes a Day of Rest

Constantine to Elpidius. All judges, city people and craftsmen shall rest on the venerable day of the Sun. But country people may without hindrance attend to agriculture . . . so that the opportunity afforded by divine providence may not be lost, for the right season is of short duration. (From the Justinian Code. Transl. in Bettenson, p. 27.) — On the introduction of Sunday as a day of rest see p. 19.

Emperors Intervene in Intra-Christian Controversies

Constantine in 326: The privileges that have been granted in consideration of religion must benefit only the adherents of the Catholic faith. It is our [imperial] will, moreover, that heretics and schismatics shall not only be alien from these privileges but shall also be bound and subjected to various compulsory public services. (*The Theodosian Code*, tr. Clyde Pharr — [Princeton: Princeton U. Pr., 1952], p. 450.)

Bishop Hosius to Emperor Constantius. . . . Cease, I implore you, from these proceedings. Remember that you are mortal and be fearful of the Day of Judgment. . . . Do not interfere in matters ecclesiastical, nor give us orders on such questions, but learn about them from us. For into your hands God has put the kingdom; the affairs of His church He has committed to us [the bishops]. . . . 'Render unto Caesar the things that are Caesar's and unto God the things that are God's.' We are not permitted to exercise an earthly rule; and you, Sire, are not authorized to burn incense. . . . (From Athanasius' *Hist. Arian.* 44, Bettenson, pp. 28 f.) — For the struggle between Catholic (orthodox) bishops and Arian emperors see p. 64. Constantius, a son of Constantine, was a fanatical Arian and did not hesitate to use violence to force recalcitrant bishops to accept Arianism. For the Arian controversy see p. 60.

Christian Bishop Versus Christian Emperor

Bp. Ambrose to Emp. Theodosius after the Thessalonian massacre of 390: 6. Something unparalleled in history has happened at Thessalonica, something which I tried in vain to prevent. Indeed, before it happened, when I was plying you with petitions against it, I said that it would be utterly atrocious; and when it happened . . . I could not extenuate it. 7. Are you ashamed, Sir, to do as David did — David, the king and prophet, the ancestor of Christ . . . who said, "I have sinned against the Lord" [II Sam. 12:1-17]. Therefore do not take it ill, Sir, if what was said to King David is said to you: "You are the [guilty] man". . . . 9. . . . That man sins is no cause for surprise. What is blameworthy is his failure to acknowledge his error and humble himself before God. . . . 11. . . . You are a man, and temptation has come to you. Conquer it. Sin is only put away by tears and penitence. . . . The Lord . . . gives remission only to those who offer penitence. . . . 13. For my part, though in all other respects I am a debtor to your goodness, for which I can never be ungrateful . . . I dare not offer the Sacrifice [of the Eucharist] if you intend to be present. Can what was not allowed when the blood of only one innocent man was shed, be allowed when the blood of many has been shed? I do not think so. 14. . . . I am writing you with my own hand for you alone to read. . . . 15. . . . "To everything there is a time" [Eccl. 3:1]. . . . You shall make your oblation when you are given permission [by me] . . . when your offering is acceptable to God. . . . 17. . . . I hold you in affection, I attend you with my prayers. If you believe me, do as I say. . . . If you do not believe me, forgive me for putting God first. . . . (*Early Latin Theology*, ed. S. L. Greenslade, Vol. 5 in *Library of Christian Classics* [LCC — Philadelphia: The Westminster Press, 1956], pp. 254-8; slightly altered.) — For Ambrose and the massacre

APPENDIX

see p. 20. Christians undergoing public penance, to which the bishop was subjecting the emperor, were not allowed to bring their offering and commune at the Eucharist. For public penance see pp. 39 ff. and 140.

NO. 2 – SACRAMENTS AND WORSHIP

Baptism

Equality in Baptism: II.13. It is certainly marvelous and contrary to expectation, but this rite does away with all difference and distinction of rank. Even if a man happens to enjoy worldly honor, if he happens to glitter with wealth, if he boasts of high lineage or the glory which is his in this world, he stands side by side with the beggar and with him who is clothed in rags. . . . Nor is he disgusted by this, because he knows that all these differences find no place in the world of the spirit. . . .

Postponing Baptism: IX.34. I count you blessed, even before you enter the sacred nuptial chamber [of the baptismal union with Christ] . . . because, unlike men of laxity, you do not approach Baptism at your final gasp. . . . 5. They receive Baptism in their beds, but you receive it in the bosom of the common mother of us all, the church; they receive Baptism amidst laments and tears, but you are baptized with rejoicing and gladness. . . . 6. . . . The dying man weeps and laments . . . , his children stand about in tears, his wife mars her cheeks with her nails. . . . 8. In the midst of such tumult and confusion the priest comes in, and his arrival is a greater source of fear than the fever itself. . . . When he enters, their despair is deeper than when the physician said he had given up all hope for the patient's life. Thus, he who is an argument for eternal life [the minister of Baptism] is seen as a symbol of death. 9. But I have not yet come to the summit of these evils. Oftentimes his soul leaps forth and deserts his body while the relatives are still raising a din . . . even though his soul brought no delight to many of them while it was still present in his body. When the man who is about to be baptized is unconscious and lies as inert as a log or stone . . . when he cannot make the responses by which he will enter into the blessed contract with the common Master of us all, what benefit does he get from his initiation?

Stripping for Baptism: XI.28. After stripping you of your robe, the priest . . . leads you down into the flowing waters. But why naked? He reminds you of your former nakedness, when you were in Paradise and you were not ashamed. For Holy Writ says: "Adam and Eve were naked and were not ashamed," until they took up the garment of sin, a garment heavy with abundant shame. 29. Do not, then, feel shame here, for the Bath is much better then the garden of Paradise.

The Many Gifts of Baptism: III.5. "Blessed be God, who alone does wondrous things" [Ps. 72:18], who makes all things and transforms them. Before yesterday you were captives, but now you are free and citizens of the church; lately you lived in the shame of your sins, but now you live in freedom and justice. You are not only free, but also holy; . . . you are not only just but also sons; not only sons, but also heirs; not only heirs, but also brothers of Christ; . . . not only joint heirs, but also members [of Christ]; not only members, but also the temple; not only the temple, but also the instrument of the [Holy] Spirit. . . . 6. You see how numerous are the gifts of Baptism. Although many men think that the only gift it confers is the remission of sins, we have counted its honors to the number of ten. It is on this account that we baptize even infants, although they are without sins,* that they may be given the further gifts of sanctification, justice, filial adoption, and inheritance, that they may be brothers and members of Christ, and become dwelling places for the [Holy] Spirit.

(* The belief that children are born with original sin was not universal.)

Baptism Makes Men Athletes of God: 8. Up to now you have been in a school for training and exercise. . . . But from today on, the arena stands open, the contest is at hand, the spectators have taken their seats. Not only are men watching the combats but the host of angels as well . . . [1 Cor. 4:9] and the Lord . . . presides over the contest as judge. This is not only an honor for us, but assures our safety . . . when the Judge of the contest is the One who laid down His life for us. (From John Chrysostom's [see p. 33] *Baptismal Instructions*, Ancient Christian Writers, Vol. 31 [Westminster, Md.: Newman Press], pp. 48, 132-4, 170, and 57-8.) — For Baptism, see pp. 34 ff.

The Eucharistic Liturgy in Jerusalem ca. 350

3. Then the deacon cries aloud: "Receive one another and let us kiss one another!" But do not think that this kiss is the same as those given in public by ordinary friends. . . . This kiss reconciles souls with one another and wins complete forgiveness. This kiss, then, is a sign of the blending of souls and the banishing of all remembrance of wrongs. For this reason Christ said: "If you are offering your gift at the altar . . . go first to be reconciled to your brother. . . ." [Matt. 5: 23-4]. The kiss, then, is one of reconciliation. . . .

4. Next, the priest cries aloud: "Lift up your hearts!" . . . Then you reply: "We have them with the Lord." . . . 5. Then the priest says: "Let us give thanks to the Lord!" . . . Then you say: "It is worthy and just." . . . 6. After this we make remembrance of heaven and earth, of sun and moon, of stars and all creation, rational and irrational, visible and invisible, of angels, archangels, . . . cherubim . . . seraphim whom Isaiah . . . beheld encircling the throne of God . . . as they sing: "Holy, holy, holy, Lord God of Sabaoth." For this reason we recite the very same hymn of God's praise, . . . that we may have fellowship with the supercosmic hosts in their hymn of praise.

7. Then, having sanctified ourselves by these spiritual hymns, we call upon God, the lover of men, to send His Holy Spirit upon the gifts that are set forth, that He may make

the bread the body of Christ and the wine the blood of Christ; for whatever the Holy Spirit shall touch is sanctified and changed.

8. Then, after the spiritual sacrifice, the bloodless worship, has been completed, upon that sacrifice of propitiation we entreat God for the common peace of the church, for the right order in the world, for kings, for soldiers and allies, for those who are burdened with sickness and overwhelmed with sorrows; in a word, we all pray and offer this sacrifice for all who stand in need of help.

9. Then we make remembrance also of those who have fallen asleep before us: first, the patriarchs, the apostles, martyrs, that at their prayers and intervention God may receive our petitions; then for . . . all who have fallen asleep from among us, believing that it will be of great advantage to these souls for whom the supplication is offered while that holy and awesome sacrifice is presented.

11. Then, after these things, we say that prayer which the Savior delivered to His own disciples . . . "Our Father . . . ."

19. After this the priest says: "Holy things to those who are holy. . . ." Then you add: "One is holy, One is Lord, Jesus Christ. . . ."

20. After this you hear the voice of the chanter inviting you with a sacred melody to the communion of the holy mysteries, as he sings: "Taste and see that the Lord is good" [Ps. 34:9]. . . .

21. As you approach, then . . . make of your left hand as if a throne for your right, which is about to receive the King, and in the hollow of your hand receive the body of Christ, replying "Amen. . . ."

22. Then, after the communion of Christ's body, approach also the cup of His blood . . . bending forward in an attitude of adoration and reverence, and saying "Amen." . . . Then wait for the prayer and give thanks to God who has deemed you worthy of such great mysteries. (From Cyril of Jerusalem's *Catechetical Lecture No. 5, Sacraments and*

Worship, Sources of Christian Theology, Vol. I, ed. Paul F. Palmer [Westminster, Md.: Newman Press, 1955], pp. 48-51; slightly altered.) — For the Eucharist see pp. 28 ff.

The "Universal Prayer"

DEACON: "Let us pray in peace to the Lord!"

PEOPLE: "Help, save, pity and defend us, O God, by Your grace!"

D.: "For the peace which comes from above, for God's good-will and for our salvation."

P.: "Lord, we pray to you."

D.: "For the peace of the whole world and for the unity of all the holy churches."

P.: "Lord, ..."

D.: "For this holy community and for the whole catholic and apostolic church, stretching from one end of the earth to the other."

P.: "Lord, ..."

D.: "For the salvation and safety of our holy patriarch ... of all the clergy and of all the Christian people."

P.: "Lord, ..."

D.: "For our ... rulers. ..."

P.: "Lord, ..."

D.: "For the holy and royal City of Christ ... and for all the cities and all the regions of the earth. ..."

P.: "Lord, ..."

D.: "For those who bring forth fruit and do beautiful things in the holy churches of God; for those who remember the poor, the widows and the orphans and the strangers; and for those who have asked us to remember them in our prayers."

P.: "Lord, ..."

THE CHURCH IN A CHANGING WORLD

D.: "For the old and the infirm, for the sick and the unfortunate. . . ."

P.: "Lord, . . ."

D.: "For all Christians who travel . . . for those who are far away from home, for our brothers who are in captivity, in exile, in prison or in bitter servitude, and for their safe return home in joy."

P.: "Lord, . . ."

D.: "For our fathers and our brothers here present, who pray with us now and at all times, that they may be full of zeal and labor with diligence."

P.: "Lord, . . ."

D.: "And for every Christian soul under trial and depression, in need of God's aid and mercy; for all who have gone astray, for the healing of the sick . . . and for the repose of our fathers and brothers who are asleep."

P.: "Lord, . . ."

D.: "We remember the most holy . . . Mother of God, . . . the saints and the blessed, the glorious John, . . . the Baptizer, the . . . apostles, Stephen, the first deacon and martyr, Moses, Aaron, Elijah. . . ."

P.: "Kyrie eleison, Kyrie eleison, Kyrie eleison!" (From the *Liturgy of St. James*, which represents the Syrian family of Eastern liturgies and is the parent of the Liturgy of St. Basil and the Liturgy of St. John Chrysostom stemming from the latter part of the 4th century and used in the Eastern Orthodox churches to this day.) — See p. 32 concerning the deacon's litany.

A Roman Collect

Guide Your church, we beseech You, Lord, by Your constant rule, that she may walk warily in time of quiet and boldly in time of trouble; for the sake of our Lord Jesus Christ

Your Son, who lives and reigns with You in the unity of the Holy Spirit in every age. Amen. (From the *Leonine Sacramentary,* a late-6th-century Roman collection of prayers, many of which are of more ancient origin. We lack, however, earlier Western liturgical books for our period.) — For the Collect see p. 33.

Early Poem

Of the Father's Love Begotten ere the worlds began to be, He is Alpha and Omega ["A" and "Z"], He the source, the ending He of the things that are And that have been and that future years shall see, Evermore and evermore.
(From the poem of Aurelius Clemens Prudentius, 348-413.)

Early Hymn

Sing, my tongue, the glorious battle, Sing the winning of the fray; Now above the cross, the trophy, Sound the loud triumphant lay: Tell how Christ, the world's Redeemer, As a victim won the day.
(1st verse of a hymn by Venantius Fortunatus, 530-609.) — For this understanding of Christ's death see pp. 54-58.

The Breast-Plate of St. Patrick

I bind unto myself today The power of God to hold and lead, His eye to watch, His might to stay, His ear to hearken to my need; The Wisdom of my God to teach, His hand to guide, His shield to ward; The Word of God to give me speech, His heavenly host to be my guard.
(From the "Hymn of St. Patrick," an Irish hymn from at least the 6th century.)

NO. 3 – PENITENTIAL DISCIPLINE

On the Necessity of Penance for the Lapsed

If in the case of lesser crimes, which are not committed against God [directly, as is apostasy] penance is done for a reasonable time and confession is made and the conduct of the penitent has been examined, nor may any [such public penitent] come to Communion unless the hand has been placed upon him by the bishop and clergy [in the act of reconciliation], how much more in the case of the most serious and deadly crimes [i. e., the denial of the faith and the relapsing into idolatry] ought everything to be arranged with caution and discretion according to the discipline of the Lord. . . . (From Cyprian's *Letter 17,* defending the need of a penitential discipline for those who lapsed in the empire-wide persecution of Christians in the mid-3rd century. Trans. from Paul F. Palmer, *Sacraments and Forgiveness, Sources of Christian Theology,* Vol. II [Westminster, Md.: Newman Press, 1959], p. 46.) — See pp. 12-13 and 34 ff. for the persecution and the penitential practices.

On the Need of Granting Forgiveness

We had decided . . . that those who had been tripped up by the Adversary in the troubled times of persecution and had lapsed and stained themselves with unlawful sacrifices, should undergo for a long time the full [public] penance, and, if danger of sickness be urgent, that the penitents should receive peace [with the church] at the point of death. For it was not right . . . that they should on departing this life be committed to the Lord without communion and peace, especially since He Himself . . . has given a law to the effect that what would be bound on earth would be bound in heaven . . . [Matt. 18:18]. But now when we see a day of further and renewed trouble [persecution] to draw near . . . we have decided that peace is to be given to those . . . who have not ceased . . . to do penance . . . that they might be armed and equipped [by receiving Communion] for the battle which is imminent. (From Cyprian's *Letter 57*, Palmer, op. cit., p. 50.)

On the Need of Both Firmness and Compassion

6. . . . O bishop, . . . judge first of all strictly, and afterwards receive [the sinner], with mercy and compassion, when he promises to repent. . . . When you have seen one who has sinned, be stern with him and command they put him out [of the congregation] . . . and take him to task . . . and then let them come in and plead for him. For our Savior Himself also was pleading with His Father for sinners. . . . And then, bishop, . . . examine him whether he is repentant. And if he is worthy to be received [back] into the church, appoint him days of fasting according to his offense, 2 or 3 weeks, or 5 or 7; and so dismiss him . . . saying to him whatever is right for admonition and instruction . . . and afterwards receive the penitent as a merciful father. . . . 7. . . . know your place, that it is that of God Almighty, and that you [O bishop] have received authority to forgive sins [Matth. 18:18]. . . . (From the 3rd century Syriac *Didascalia Apostolorum* — Teaching of the Apostles — tr. and ed. R. H. Connolly, [Oxford: Clarendon Press, 1929], pp. 40 ff.; slightly altered.)

The Graded Penitential Discipline

Canon 7. Those who have enrolled among the barbarians, and, . . . forgetful that they are Pontians and Christians, become so barbarized as even to put to death by the gibbet or by strangulation those of their own people, and to point out to the barbarians their [people's] way of escape or their houses, such you must exclude even from [the grade of] "hearer," until a common decision as to what should be done with them is reached by the saints. . . .

Canon 8. With regard to those who have dared to break into the houses of others during the plundering raids of the barbarians . . . they are to be unworthy even of the "hearing" [grade]; but if they declare themselves and make restitution, they are to be "fallers" in the ranks of the penitents.

Canon 9. But those who have found [and kept for themselves] . . . something [stolen and] left behind by the barbarians, . . . they are likewise to be placed among the "fallers"; but if they declare themselves and make restitution, they are to be deemed worthy even of the prayer [i. e., they may, apparently, stay for the "prayer of the faithful" which took place after the dismissal of the catechumens and of the rest of penitents].

Canon 11. The grade of "mourner" takes place outside the door of the church; here it is proper for the sinner to stand and to beseech the faithful as they enter to pray for him. That of the "hearer" is inside the door, in the narthex; here it is proper for the sinner to stand as long as the catechumens remain, and then leave [with them]. For he [Gregory] says, that when such one has heard the Scriptures and the instructions, let him be led out and not be counted worthy of the prayer. The grade of the "faller" is had when he stands within the door of the nave [where the faithful are assembled], and leaves with the catechumens. That of "bystander," when he takes his stand with the faithful [in the nave] and does not have to leave with the catechumens. Last is that of "participant" [communicant] in the Holies. (From *The Canonical Epistle* [Palmer, pp. 64 f.; slightly altered], describing the disciplinary proceedings in Pontus, Asia Minor, which underwent a barbarian invasion ca. 260. Except for canon 11, the canons are found in the letter of Gregory the Wonderworker [*Thaumatourgos*] to a fellow bishop in the area. Gregory had converted the population of Pontus to Christianity, an example of an early mass-conversion. The conversion had evidently involved some rather surface understanding of Christianity. The sins described here are unusual for the early church.)

Irish Penitential Canons

13. Whoever shall commit homicide, that is, shall slay his neighbor, let him do penance on bread and water for three years, in exile and unarmed, and after 3 years let him come back to his own, rendering to the parents of the one slain and in his stead filial reverence and service; and thus satisfaction having been made let him be joined [admitted] to the altar by the judgment of the priest.

20. If any layman shall commit perjury . . . through greed, let him sell all his goods and give to the poor and let him be converted to the Lord, and . . . giving up everything of the world, let him serve God in a monastery until death. . . .

30. Now it is prescribed that confessions be made diligently, especially with regard to disturbances of the soul, before one goes to Mass, lest perchance one approach the altar unworthily. For it is better to wait until the heart is sound and a stranger to scandal and envy than to proceed boldly to the judgment of the tribunal . . . the altar of Christ. . . . (From *The Penitential of Columban,* ca. 600, Palmer, pp. 143 ff.) — Columban was an Irish missionary to France. For the Irish contribution see pp. 111 ff.

NO. 4 — FAITH AND TEACHING

Athanasius: The Incarnation of the Word of God

The Tie Between Creation and Redemption: 1. . . . we have indicated that the Word of the Father is Himself Divine, that all things that are owe their being to His will and power, and that it is through Him that the Father gives order to creation, and that by Him all things are moved. . . . For the first thing you must grasp is this: the renewal of creation has been wrought by the Self-same Word who made it in the beginning. There is thus no inconsistency between creation and salvation; for the one Father has employed the same Agent for both works, effecting the salvation of the world through the same Word who made it in the beginning.

4. Men, having turned from the contemplation of God to evil of their own devising, had come inevitably under the law of death. . . . As they had at the beginning come into being out of non-existence, so were they now on the way to returning, through corruption, to non-existence again. The presence and love of the Word had called them into being; inevitably therefore, when they lost the knowledge of God they lost existence with it. . . . 5. . . . Though they were by nature subject to corruption, the grace of their union with the Word had made them capable of escaping the natural law [of death] . . . "but by envy of the devil death entered the world" [Wisdom 2:24]. When this happened, men began to die and corruption ran riot among them, gaining even more than its natural power over the whole race . . . for, having invented wickedness in the beginning and so involving themselves in death and corruption, they had gone on gradually from bad to worse. . . . Adulteries and thefts were everywhere, murder and plundering filled the earth, law was disregarded in corruption and injustice . . . nations were rising against nations and the whole earth was rent with factions and battles. . . .

6. As [men] such noble works [of God] were on the road to ruin, what then was God, being good, to do? . . . 7. . . . What was it that was needed for a reversal of the situation? What save the Word of God Himself who also at the beginning had made all things out of nothing? . . . For He alone . . . was both able to recreate all and worthy to suffer on behalf of all and to be an ambassador for all with the Father. 8. For this purpose, then, the incorporeal and incorruptible and immaterial Word of God entered our world. In one sense, indeed, He was not far from it before

for no part of creation had ever been without Him. . . . But now He entered the world in a new way, stooping to our level in His love and Self-revealing to us. . . . Thus, taking a body like our own, because all our bodies are liable to the corruption of death, He surrendered His body to death instead of all, and offered it to the Father. This He did out of sheer love for us, so that in His death all might die, and that the law of death might thereby be abolished because, having fully spent its power in the Lord's body, it was thereafter voided of its power over men. . . . 9. . . . Through this union of the immortal Son of God with our human nature, all men were clothed with incorruption in the promise of the resurrection. . . . 10. . . . By man death has gained power over men; by the Word made man death has been destroyed and life raised up anew [1 Cor. 15:21 ff.]. . . . Now therefore when we die we no longer do so as men condemned to death but as those who are even now in the process of rising we await the general resurrection of all, "which at the proper time He shall make manifest" [1 Tim. 6:15]. . . . This, then, is the first cause of the Savior's becoming man. There are, however, also other things which show how fitting is His blessed presence in our midst and these we must now go on to consider.

God's Self-Revelation: 11. God, . . . when He was making the race of men through His Word saw . . . that it was not able of itself to know its Maker, nor to get any idea at all of God, the Incorporeal and Uncreate. He took pity on them, therefore, and did not leave them destitute of the knowledge of Himself. . . . Thus the good God has given them a share in His own Image, our Lord Jesus Christ, and makes them in His own Image and in His Likeness: so that through the gift of God-likeness in themselves they may be able to perceive the Image Absolute, that is, the Word of the Father and through Him get an idea of the Father, and, knowing their Maker, live the happy and truly blessed life. But, as we have already seen, men, foolish as they are, thought little of the grace they had received and turned away from God. They defiled their own soul so completely that they not only lost their idea of God but invented for themselves other gods of various kinds. . . . Yet He had not given the knowledge of Himself only in one way; but rather He had unfolded it in many forms and by many ways. 12. He provided the works of creation also as a means by which the Maker might be known. . . . He gave them the Law and sent them the prophets. . . . Yet men . . . did not lift up their heads towards the truth. . . . 13. What was God to do in face of this dehumanizing of mankind? . . . Therefore He took a human body, that while death might once for all be destroyed in it, men might be renewed according to the Image. . . . 14. You know what happens when a portrait that has been painted on a panel becomes obliterated through external stains. The artist does not throw the panel away, but the subject of the portrait has to come and sit for it again, and then the likeness is re-drawn on the same material. Even so it was with the All-holy Son of God. He, the Image of the Father, came and dwelt in our midst that He might renew mankind once made in His likeness. . . .

15. . . . Men had turned from the contemplation of God above and were looking in the opposite direction. . . . So the Savior of us all, the Word of God, in His great love assumed a body and moved as Man among men; and through His actions done in that body, as it were on their own level, He teaches those who would not learn by other means to know Himself, the Word of God, and through Him, the Father. He deals with them as a good teacher with his pupils, coming down to their level and using simple means. . . . 17. . . . He was not, as might be imagined, hedged in by His body. . . . At one and the same time—this is the wonder—as Man He was living a human life, and as Word He was sustaining the life of the universe, and as Son He was in constant union with the Father. . . .

Living Proofs of Christ's Conquest of Death and His Deity
27. A very strong proof of the destruction of death and of its having been conquered by the Cross is supplied by a

present fact, namely this. All the disciples of Christ scorn death; they take offensive against it and, instead of fearing it, by the sign of the cross and by faith in Christ trample on it as on something dead . . . and prefer to die rather than to deny their faith in Christ. . . . "O Death, where is your victory? O grave, where is your sting? [1 Cor. 15:55]. 30. . . . Dead men cannot take effective action. . . . Well then, look at the facts of the case. The Savior is working mightily among men; every day He is invisibly persuading numbers of people all over the world . . . to accept His faith and be obedient to His teaching. Can anyone, in face of this, still doubt that He is risen and lives, or rather that He Himself is the Life? . . . If He is dead, how is it that He makes the living cease from their [accustomed] activities, the adulterer from his adultery, the murderer from his murdering, the unjust from avarice, while the profane and godless man becomes religious? . . . 50. . . . Whose death ever drove out demons, or whose death did ever demons fear, save that of Christ? For where the Savior is named, there every demon is driven out. Again, who has ever so rid men of their natural passions that . . . those who formerly were craven cowards boldly play the man? And in short, what persuaded the barbarians and heathen folk . . . to give heed to peace, save the faith of Christ and the sign of the Cross? . . . 52. Who, then, is He who has done these things and has united in peace those who hated each other, save the beloved Son of the Father, the common Savior of all, Jesus Christ, who by His own love underwent all things for our salvation? . . . 55. . . . Now this is proof that Christ is God, the Word and Power of God. For whereas human things cease and the Word of Christ remains, it is clear to all eyes that the things which cease are temporary, but that He who abides is God and very Son of God, the Only-begotten Word. (From Athanasius, *On the Incarnation of the Word of God* [New York: Macmillan Co., 1946 trans., slightly alt.], pp. 25 f., 29-43, 45, 57 f., 60 f., 89, 90.) — For Athanasius and the faith he represents see pp. 56 f. and 61 f.

Arius: Christ Is Quite Different from God

These then are those who have become apostates: Arius, Achillas. . . . What they assert, in utter contrariety to the Scriptures and wholly of their own devising, is as follows: "God was not always a father . . . the Word was not from eternity, but was made out of nothing. . . ," "The Son is a creature and a work [of the Father]; He is neither like the Father in essence, nor is by nature either the Father's true Word or His true Wisdom, but indeed one of His works and creatures, being only *called* "Word" and "Wisdom," since He came into being by God's own Word and Wisdom. . . ." "The 'Word' is alien to, foreign to, and excluded from the essence of God; and the Father is invisible to the Son; for neither does the Son perfectly and accurately know the Father, nor can He perfectly behold Him. The Son does not know even the nature of His own essence; for He has been made for us, in order that God might create us by Him, as by an instrument; nor would He have ever existed had God not wished to create us." (Socrates, *Eccl. Hist.* I.6.8-11.)

He that is without beginning made the Son a beginning of things originated and advanced Him as a Son to Himself by adoption. . . . The Son is not equal, no, nor of one essence with Him. . . . Foreign from the Son in essence is the Father, for He is without beginning. . . . To speak in brief, God is ineffable to His Son. For He is to Himself what He is, that is, unspeakable. . . . For it is impossible for Him to investigate the Father, who is by Himself. . . . For it is plain that it is impossible for someone who has a beginning to conceive of someone without a beginning, or even to grasp the idea. (From Arius' poem *Thalia* as quoted by Athanasius. The two texts reproduced here are from J. Stevenson, op. cit., pp. 342-3 and 350-1, respectively.) — For Arius and his controversy with the Athanasian forces see pp. 60 ff. His teaching was rejected by the ecumenical councils which produced the Nicene Creed. See pp. 62 ff.

The Mystery of God

You are revealed, Lord, to babes and hidden from the cunning. You are found by him who believes and hidden to him who searches. (St. Ephrem the Syrian, in his *Fourth Rhythm*, 7, ca. 370. From *Saint Ephrem the Syrian*, trans. by J. B. Morris [London: F. J. Rivington, 1847]). — St. Ephrem, the poet of Syriac-speaking Christendom, balanced the speculative interests of Greek theology with his emphasis on the mystery of God. He exercised an important influence on Byzantine hymnology.

The Savior of Men Had to Be Fully Human

If anyone has put his trust in Christ as a Man without a human mind [as the Apollinarians did] he is really bereft of mind and quite unworthy of salvation. For that which He has not taken up He has not healed; but that which is united to His Godhead is also saved. If only half Adam fell, then Christ could also have taken up and saved only half [of the human nature]; but if the whole of his nature fell, the whole human nature must be united to the whole nature of the Son of God, and so be saved as a whole. Let them not, then begrudge us our complete salvation, or clothe the Savior only with bones and nerves and the outward traits of humanity.... How is Christ man if He is without a human mind, for man is not a mindless animal! ... But, says he who proposes this [Appollinarian view] the Godhead took the place of the human intellect in Christ. How does this **touch me? For Godhead joined to flesh alone is not man,** nor to soul alone, nor to both apart from the intellect, which is the most essential part of man. Keep then the whole man and mingle Godhead with it, that you may benefit me in my completeness.... It was the mind of Adam ... which received the command and failed to keep it ... and that which transgressed was that which stood most in need of salvation; and that which needed salvation was what He also took upon Him. (From Gregory of Nazianzen's anti-Apollinarian **Letter 51, to Cledonius.** *Nicene and Post-Nicene Fathers,* 2nd series, Vol. VII [Christian Literature Co.: New York, 1894], pp. 440-1, slightly alt.) — For the Apollinarian controversy see pp. 68 ff.

The Incarnation Is Not Unworthy of God

24. That the omnipotent nature was capable of descending to man's lowly position is a clearer evidence of power than great and supernatural miracles. For it somehow accords with God's nature, and is consistent with it, to do great and sublime things by divine power. . . . But descent to man's lowly position is a supreme example of power — of a power which is not bounded by circumstances contrary to its nature. . . . We marvel at the way the sublime entered a state of lowliness, and while actually seen in it, did not leave the heights. We marvel at the way the Godhead was entwined in human nature and, while becoming man, did not cease to be God. . . .

27. . . . [As for objections to God's uniting Himself with human nature as something unworthy of the sublime God:] Indeed, if it is permissible to conceive of anything, except evil, as unworthy of God, such a situation is as **unworthy of Him as any other.** . . . **For every created thing is** *equally* inferior to the Most High who, because of His transcendent nature, is unapproachable. . . . If then everything equally falls short of this dignity, the one thing which really befits God's nature still remains, namely, to come to the aid of those in need. . . .

28. But our opponents ridicule human nature, and keep stressing the [presumably unworthy] manner of our birth. . . . But . . . evil, and what is akin to it, are alone essentially shameful. The whole course of our nature has been arranged by God's will and law, and hence it is far removed

from the censure of evil. Otherwise the condemnation of our nature would reflect upon the Creator, if any aspect of it could be charged with being disgraceful or improper. The only thing alien to the Divine is evil. Nature is not evil. (From Gregory of Nyssa's *Address on Religious Instruction, LCC 3*, pp. 300-1 and 304-6.) — See also pp. 60 ff.

Nestorius: The Deity and Humanity of Christ Have to Be Kept Distinct!

2. . . . Certain ones of our clergy . . . openly blaspheme God the Word . . . as if He took His beginning from the Christ-bearing Virgin and grew up with His [bodily] temple and was buried with it. . . . They do not scruple to call the Christ-bearing Virgin *Theotokos* [God-bearer]. . . . We say that this word is not appropriate for her who gave birth [to His humanity], since a true mother is of the same essence as what is born of her [and she does not have the same essence as the Divine Word]. But the term could be accepted in consideration of this, that the word would be used of the Virgin only because of the inseparable temple of God the Word which was of her [i. e., because the 'temple' to which she gave birth is inseparable from the Word], not because she is the mother of the Word — for no one gives birth to one older than oneself. (From Nestorius' *Letter to Celestine, LCC 3*, pp. 347-8.) — For Nestorius see pp. 69 ff.

Cyril: The Indivisibility of Christ's Deity from His Humanity

We confess that He who was begotten from God the Father . . . though He is by His own proper nature not subject to suffering, suffered in the flesh for us, according to the Scriptures, and was . . . impassibly making His own the suffering of His own flesh. . . .

We must necessarily add this: proclaiming the death in the flesh of the unique Son of God . . . and His return to life from the dead and His reception into heaven, we celebrate the . . . service in the churches. So we approach the mystical gifts [the Eucharist] and are sanctified, becoming partakers of the holy flesh and the honorable blood of Christ the Savior of all . . . receiving it . . . as the Word's own flesh and truly Life-giving. For the Word being by nature, as God, Life, when He had become one with His flesh, He made it Life-giving. . . .

We do not divide the terms used in the Gospels of the Savior [referring some merely to His humanity and others merely to His Deity]. . . . All the terms used in the Gospels are to be referred to one Person, the one incarnate *hypostasis* of the Word. There is one Lord Jesus Christ, according to the Scriptures. . . . Since the holy Virgin gave birth after the flesh to God who was united by *hypostasis* with flesh, therefore we say that she is *Theotokos* [God-bearer], not as though the nature of the Word had the beginning of its existence from the flesh. (From the 3rd letter of Cyril to Nestorius, *LCC* 3, pp. 351-2, slightly alt.) — **For the Christological controversy, the term "Theotokos," usually translated as "Mother of God," and the teaching of Cyril, see pp. 70 ff. The Greek word** *hypostasis* **is untranslatable. It means that which exists in its own right; that which doesn't have a borrowed existence.**

The Paradox: The Reality and Unity of Christ's Humanity and Deity

3. . . . **While the distinctness of both natures and** substances is preserved and both meet in one Person, lowliness is assumed by majesty, weakness by power, mortality by eternity; and in order to pay the debt of our condition, the inviolable nature has been united to the nature subject to suffering. . . . Therefore, in the entire and perfect nature of very Man was born very God, whole in what was His, whole in what was ours. . . . Each of the natures retains its proper character without defect. . . . 4. . . . For the Selfsame who is very God is also very Man: and there is no illusion in this union, while the lowliness of man and the loftiness of God meet together. For as God is not changed by the

compassion [exhibited], so manhood is not swallowed up by the majesty. Each aspect [of Christ's person] does the acts which belong to it, in communion with the other: that is, the Word performing what belongs to the Word, and the flesh carrying out what belongs to the flesh. . . . 5. . . . On account of the unity which is to be understood as existing between the two natures . . . the Son of God is said to have been crucified and buried, although this did not pertain to His Divinity as such. . . .

This is the faith by which the catholic church lives and advances, namely, that in Christ Jesus . . . there is neither a humanity without real Divinity nor Divinity without real humanity. (From Leo's *Tome* [see p. 72], condemning the assertions of a certain confused abbot, Eutyches, who could not see how Christ could be truly man if He was God. Trans. from *LCC* 3, pp. 363-6 and 368, slightly alt.)

Following the holy fathers, we all with one accord teach men to acknowledge one and the same Son, our Lord Jesus Christ, as one complete in Godhead and complete in manhood, truly God and truly man . . . like us in all respects except for sin; as regards His Godhead, begotten of His Father before the ages, but yet as regards His manhood begotten for us men and our salvation of Mary the Virgin, the God-bearer [*Theotokos*]; one and the same Christ, Son, Lord, Only-begotten, recognized in two natures, without confusion, without change, without division, without separation; the distinction of natures being in no way annulled by the union, but rather the characteristics of each nature being preserved and coming together to form one person and subsistence [*hypostasis*] . . . the Lord Jesus Christ. (From the *Definition of the Faith* by the Council of Chalcedon, Bettenson, *Documents,* pp. 72 f.) — For this Council see pp. 72 ff.

On the Divine Work of the Holy Spirit

It is through the Spirit that we are all said to be "partakers of God" [2 Peter 1:4]. For it says [in 1 Cor. 3:16]:

"Do you not know that you are a temple of God and that the Spirit of God dwells in you?". . . . If the Holy Spirit were a creature, we should have no participation of God in the Spirit.[1] If indeed we were joined to a spirit which is a creature, we should be strangers to the divine nature, for we would not have a part in it. But as it is, the fact of our being called partakers of Christ and partakers of God shows that the anointing and the seal [of the Holy Spirit] that is in us belongs . . . to the nature of the Son who, through the Spirit who is in Him, joins us to the Father. This John taught us . . . when he wrote: "By this we know that we abide in God and He in us, because He has given us His own Spirit" [1 John 4:13]. But if, by participation in the Spirit, we are made "partakers of the divine nature" [2 Pet. 1:4], we should be mad to say that the Spirit has a created nature and not the nature of God. . . . If He [the Spirit] makes men divine, it is beyond doubt that His nature is the nature of God. (From Athanasius' *1st Ep. to Bp. Serapion,* Ch. 24, *Letters of St. Athanasius Concerning the Holy Spirit,* C. R. B. Shapland, ed., [New York: Philosophical Library, 1951], pp. 125-7. Slightly alt.) — For the controversy regarding the Holy Spirit see pp. 65 f. above.

NO. 5 — THE BISHOPS AND THE CHURCH

Cyprian: The Apostolic Authority of Bishops and the Church's Unity

Our Lord . . . establishes the honorable rank of bishop and the constitution of His church when in the Gospel He speaks and says to Peter: "I say to you: You are

---

[1] Cf. Gregory of Nyssa: "Why do they [those who deny the deity of the Spirit] make war on their own Life [in Christ]? Why exclude themselves from union with God?" (*Adv. Mac.* 23, cited in *Letters of St. Athan.*, p. 216, n. 3.)

APPENDIX

Peter and upon this rock I will build my church. . . . And I will give to you the Keys of the Kingdom of heaven. And whatever you shall bind on earth shall be bound also in heaven [Matt. 16:18-19]. . . . Thence have come down to us in course of time and by due succession the ordained office of the bishop and the constitution of the church, forasmuch as the church is founded upon the bishops and every act of the church is subject to these rulers. (From Cyprian's *Epistle* 33.1, J. Quasten, *Patrology*, Vol. II, [Westminster, Md.: Newman Press, 1953], pp. 374 f.)

The church, which is catholic and one, is not split asunder nor divided but is truly bound and joined together by the cement of its priests [bishops], who hold fast one to another. (Cypr. *Ep.* 66, 8, ibid.)

It is on one man [Peter] that He builds the church, and although He assigns a like power to all the apostles after His resurrection [John 20:21 ff.] . . . yet in order that the oneness [of the church] might be unmistakable, He established by His own authority a source for that oneness having its origin in one man alone. . . . The church forms a unity, however far she spreads and multiplies . . . just as a tree's branches are many, yet the strength deriving from its sturdy root is one. So too, though many streams flow from a single spring . . . their oneness abides by reason of their starting point. . . .

Whoever breaks with the church [the "spouse of Christ"] . . . is an alien. . . . You cannot have God for your Father if you do not have the church for your mother. If there was escape for anyone who was outside the ark of Noah, there is escape too for one who is found outside the church. (From Cyprian's famed *On the Unity of the Church*, 4-6, trans. by Maurice Bevenot, in *St. Cyprian, The Lapsed and The Unity of the Church*, ACW, Vol. 25, 1957, pp. 45-47.) —Cyprian's treatise was written in the mid-3rd century to defend the unity of the church and the authority of the bishops against schismatics. For Cyprian see pp. 91 f. See also his statement on the need of church discipline, pp. 140 f., reflecting the middle-of-the-road position of the church contrasted with the extreme leniency or rigorism of the schismatics.

NO. 6 – PHYSICIANS OF THE SOUL

Pastoral Care

27. . . . The healers of our bodies will have their labors and vigils and cares . . . and will reap a harvest of pain for themselves from the distresses of others, as one of their wise men said. . . .

28. But we, upon whose efforts is staked the salvation of the soul . . . what a struggle ought ours to be, and how great skill do we need to treat, or get men treated properly, and to change their life. . . . For, men and women, young and old, rich and poor, the sanguine and the despondent, the sick and those who are well, the rulers and the ruled, the wise and the ignorant, the cowardly and courageous, the wrathful and the meek, the successful and the failing, do not require the same instruction and encouragement. . . .

30. As then the same medicine and the same food are not administered to men, but a difference is made according to their degree of health or infirmity, so also are souls treated with varying instructions and guidance. . . . Some are led best by teaching, others by example; some need the spur, others the curb. . . .

31. Some are benefited by praise, others by criticism, both being applied at the right time; while if applied at the wrong time or in an unreasonable way, the application does harm to them. Some are set right by encouragement, others by rebuke; some when taken to task in public, others when privately corrected. For some tend to disregard private admonitions but are recalled to their senses by the condemnation of a number of people, while others, who would grow reckless under reproof openly given, accept rebuke because it is in secret, and yield obedience in return for sympathy.

APPENDIX

32. Upon some it is needful to keep close watch, even in the minutest details, because if they think they are unperceived (as they would contrive to be) they are puffed up with the idea of their own cleverness. Of others it is better to take no notice, but "seeing not to see, and hearing not to hear them," according to the proverb, that we may not drive them to despair under the depressing influence of repeated reproofs, and at last to utter recklessness, when they have lost the sense of self-respect, the source of persuasiveness [literally, the medicine of persuasion]. In some cases we must even be angry, without feeling angry, or treat them with disdain we do not actually feel, or manifest despair, though we do not really despair of them, according to the needs of their nature. Others again we must treat with great fairness and gentleness, helping them readily to conceive a hope of their being able to improve. . . .

33. . . . Instead of one and the same medicine invariably proving either most wholesome or most dangerous in the same cases—be it severity or gentleness, or any of the others which we have enumerated—in some cases it proves good and useful, in others again it has the contrary effect, according, I suppose, to the time and circumstances and the disposition of the patient. Now to set before you the distinction between all these things, and give you a perfectly exact overview of them, so that you may in brief comprehend the medical art, is quite impossible, even for one qualified in the highest degree by care and skill; but they become clear by actual experience and practice. . . .

74. I know whose servants we are, and where we are placed, and whither we are guides. I know the height of God, and the weakness of man, and, on the contrary, His power. . . .

78. . . . The commission to guide and govern souls is too high for me . . . [and this is why I tried to flee the office].

113. . . . [But] God in His goodness rewards our trust [in Him] and makes a perfect ruler [pastor] of the man who

has confidence in Him and places all his hopes in Him. (From Gregory Nazianzen's *In Defense of His Flight* [from the pastoral office], trans. by C. G. Brown and J. E. Swallow in *N & PNF,* 2nd series, Vol. VII, 1894, pp. 210-11 and 220, slightly alt.) — Gregory composed this treatise after he returned to his post at Nazianzus, from which he had fled after his father, a bishop, had forcibly ordained him. Gregory explains the awesome responsibilities of the pastoral office which had made him flee from it. See pp. 85 ff. above for the tasks. The treatise had an enormous influence on all future treatments of the pastoral work. Gregory the Great's *Pastoral Rule* (see pp. 94 ff.) is a development of the above theme.

NO. 7 — CHRISTIAN OUTREACH TO A PAGAN WORLD

Toward the Conversion of the Angles

When Almighty God shall have brought you to our most reverend brother the bishop Augustine, tell him that I have long been considering with myself about the case of the Angli; to wit, that the temples of idols in that nation should not be destroyed, but that the idols themselves that are in them should be. Let blessed water be prepared, and sprinkled in these temples, and altars constructed, and relics deposited, since, if these same temples are well built, it is needful that they should be transferred from the worship of idols to the service of the true God; that, when the people themselves see that these temples are not destroyed, they may put away error from their heart, and, knowing and adoring the true God, may have recourse with the more familiarity to the places they have been accustomed to. And, since they are wont to kill many oxen in sacrifice to demons, they should have also some solemnity of this kind in a changed form, so that on the day of dedication, or on the anniversaries of the holy martyrs whose relics are deposited there, they may make for themselves tents of the branches of trees around these temples that have been changed into churches, and celebrate the solemnity with religious feasts. Nor let them any longer sacrifice animals to the devil, but slay animals to the praise of God for their own eating, and return thanks to the Giver of all for their fulness, so that, while some joys are reserved to them outwardly, they may be able the more easily to incline their minds to inward joys. For it is undoubtedly impossible to cut away everything at once from hard hearts, since one who strives to ascend to the highest place must needs rise by steps or paces, and not by leaps. Thus to the people of Israel in Egypt the Lord did indeed make Himself known; but still He reserved to them in His own worship the use of the sacrifices which they were accustomed to offer to the devil, enjoining them to immolate animals in sacrifice to Himself; to the end that, their hearts being changed, they should omit some things in the sacrifice and retain others, so that, though the animals were the same as what they had been accustomed to offer, nevertheless, as they immolated them to God and not to idols, they should be no longer the same sacrifices. (From Gregory the Great's letter to Mellitus, Book XI, Ep. 76 in *N & PNF*, 2nd series, Vol. XIII, p. 85.) — The letter was intended for the missionaries whom Gregory had dispatched to convert the heathen Angles. It shows the philosophy which succeeded in winning the pagan world (see p. 83).

NO. 8 — THE MONASTIC LEAVEN

The Experience of the Desert

IV. 3. Abba Arsenius said: "An hour's sleep is enough for a monk; that is, if he is a fighter."

13. They told of Abba Dioscorus of Namisias, that ... every year he made a particular resolution: not to meet anyone for a year, or not to speak, or not to taste cooked food, or not to eat any fruit, or not to eat vegetables. This was his system in everything. He made himself master of one thing, and then started on another, and so on each year.

V.16. An old man said: ". . . We cannot make temptations vanish, but we can struggle against them."

IV.25. [Abba Cassian] said: "Abba Moses told us what Abba Serapion said to him: 'While I was still a lad, I was staying with Abba Theonas; and after each meal I was moved by some demon and I stole one of the rolls . . . and secretly ate it. . . . For some time I went on with this, until the sin began to dominate my mind and I could not stop myself. Only my conscience judged me, for I was ashamed to say anything to the old man. But by God's mercy it happened that some visitors came to the old man in search of profit to their soul, and they asked him about their own souls. The old man replied: "Nothing harms the monk so much . . . as when he conceals his thoughts from his fathers in the spirit." And he also talked to them about self-control. And while he was speaking, I thought to myself that God had revealed to him what I had done. Stricken in my heart, I began to weep; then I pulled the roll . . . out of my dress, threw myself on the floor, and begged for forgiveness for what I had done, and for prayer that I might be helped not to do it again.

Then the old man said: "My son, you are freed from your captivity . . . by your . . . confession. The demon which by your silence you let dwell in your heart, has been killed because you confessed your sin. . . . Henceforth he shall never make a home in you, because you have thrown him into the open air."

V. 3. Abba Cassian said: "Abba Moses told us: 'It is good not to hide one's thoughts but to disclose them to discreet and devout men; but not to men who are old merely in years, for many have found final despair instead of comfort by confessing to men whom they saw to be aged, but who in fact were inexperienced.'"

V.4. There was once a brother who . . . being sore troubled by the demon of lust came to an old man and told him his thoughts. The old man was inexperienced; and when he heard he was indignant, and said to the brother . . . that

APPENDIX

he is unworthy of his monk's habit, because he conceived thoughts like that. When the brother heard this, he despaired of himself, left his cell and started on his way back to the world. But by God's providence, Abba Apollos met him. And seeing him disturbed and melancholy, he asked him, "Son, why are you so sad?" The brother, much embarrassed, at first did not say a word. But when the old man pressed him . . . he confessed [what had happened]. . . . When Father Apollos heard this, he went on asking questions like a wise doctor and advised him thus: "Do not be cast down, nor despair of yourself. Even at my age and experience of the spiritual life, I am still sorely troubled by thoughts like yours. Do not fail at this point, because this trouble cannot be cured by our efforts, but only by God's mercy. Grant me what I ask, just today, and go back to your cell."

The brother obeyed him. But Abba Apollos went away to the cell of the old man who had made him desperate. He stood outside of the cell and prayed the Lord with tears and said: "Lord, who allowest men to be tempted for their good, transfer the war which that brother is suffering to this old man; let him learn by experience in his old age what many years have not taught him, and so let him find out how to sympathize with people undergoing this kind of temptation." [And his prayer was granted.]

V.5. When Abba Cyrus of Alexandria was asked about the temptation of lust, he said: "If you are not tempted . . . it is because you are used to sinning. The man who does not fight sin at the stage of temptation sins in his body. And the man who sins in his body has no trouble from temptation."

(From *The Sayings of the Father, LCC,* Vol. 12, trans. Owen Chadwick, pp. 49-50, 52, 60-2, 64, slightly alt.) — For the Desert Fathers see pp. 102 f.

16. Germanus: "How is it that idle thoughts creep into our minds when we do not want them or are unaware of them, so that it is quite difficult even to understand them, let alone drive them away? Is it possible for a mind to avoid delusions like this?"

17. [Abba] Moses: "Thoughts inevitably besiege the mind. But any earnest person has the power to accept or reject them. Their origin is in some way outsides ourselves, but whether to chose them or not lies within us. But because I said it was impossible for thoughts not to come to the mind, you must not put all the blame upon the spirits who assault our integrity. Otherwise the will of man would not be free, and we could make no effort for our improvement. To a great extent we have the capacity to better the sort of thoughts we receive, to let holy thoughts or secular thoughts grow into our minds. This is the purpose of reading the Bible often and meditating upon it always, to attain a higher state of recollection. . . . This is the purpose of constancy in vigils or fasts or prayer, so that the mind, in its weakened body, may care nothing for the world but may contemplate the things of heaven. If we neglect these, the mind will surely creep back towards squalid sin and fall." (From Cassian's — and his friend Germanus' — first conference with the famed desert father Moses. Quoted from *LCC,* Vol. 12, p. 207.) — Cassian, who had spent years in the Egyptian desert and then founded a monastery in Marseilles, was both a mediator and source of Eastern wisdom for Western monasticism. His *Conferences,* published ca. 425, became extremely popular in the medieval monasteries. See also pp. 97, 99, and 159-61.

St. Jerome: The Vocation of a Virgin

1.2. It is not enough for you to go out from your native country, unless you forget your people and your father's house [following Abraham, though in a figurative way] and, despising the flesh, are united in your Bridegroom's (Christ's) embraces. . . . It is not profitable, after putting one's hand to the plow, to look back [Luke 9:62]. . . .

2.1. . . . I am now not about . . . to enumerate the disadvantages of wives: pregnancy, a wailing infant, the torment of a husband's unfaithfulness, household cares, and how death at last cuts off all fancied blessings. . . . But I would have you understand that as you go out from Sodom, you must be warned by the fate of Lot's wife [Gen. 19:26]. . . .

6.6. . . . Because it is impossible for a man's senses to escape being assailed by the well-known inner passion, that man is praised . . . who as soon as he begins to cherish such thoughts stifles his imaginings and dashes them against the rock. "And the rock is Christ." [1 Cor. 10:4]

7.1. How often, when I was established in the desert and in that vast solitude which is scorched by the sun's heat and affords a savage habitation for monks, did I think myself amid the delights of Rome! . . .

7.2. I was surrounded by dancing girls [in my imagination]! My face was pale from fasting, and my mind was hot with desire. . . .

8.1. If those who with emaciated frame are assailed by their thoughts alone, endure such trials, what must a girl endure who is thrilled by luxuries [in Rome]?

16.1. I do not want you to consort with married women. . . . I do not want you to see frequently what you disdained in your desire to be a [life-long] virgin. . . . Why do you, the bride of God, make haste to call on the wife of a mortal man? Attain a holy pride in this relationship.

16.2. Know that you are better than they. . . .

17.4. It is hard for the human soul not to love, and it is necessary that our mind be drawn into some sort of affection. Love of the flesh is overcome by love of the spirit. Desire is quenched by desire.

20.1. I praise marriage . . . but I do so because wedlock produces virgins. I gather roses from thorns, gold from the earth, the pearl from the shell.

25.1. Let the secret retreat of your bedchamber ever guard you. Always let the Bridegroom [Christ] hold conversation with you within. . . . When sleep comes upon you . . . He "will put His hand through the opening and touch your body" [Song of Sol. 5:4]. You will arise, trembling, and will say: "I languish with love [for You]." [Ibid. 5:8]

40.1. Nothing is hard for lovers. No effort is difficult

for one who is passionately eager. See how much Jacob endured for Rachel, his affianced wife [Gen. 29:20]. . . . Let us also love Christ . . . and we shall find that every difficult thing is easy. (From Jerome's *Letter 22*, to Eustochium, the first high-ranking Roman lady to have vowed virginity. Excerpted from *The Letters of St. Jerome*, I, *ACW*, Vol. 33, pp. 134, 135, 139, 140-1, 147, 149, 152, 158, 177.) — For Jerome and his asceticism see pp. 105 ff.

St. Basil: An Introduction to the Ascetical Life

Noble are the ordinances decreed by a king for his ordinary subjects, but nobler and more regal are the commands he addresses to his soldiers. Therefore, let the man who wishes to be Christ's comrade in battle give ear to these words as if they were military orders: "If any man will serve me, let him follow me; and where I am, there also shall my servant be" [John 12:26]. Where is Christ the King? In heaven, to be sure. There, soldier [of Christ], you should direct your course. Forget all earthly delights. A soldier does not build a house; he does not aspire to the possession of lands; he does not concern himself with devious, money-chasing business. . . . [2 Tim. 2:4]. The soldier enjoys a sustenence provided by the king . . . he need not vex himself in this regard. By royal edict, a home lies open to him wherever there are subjects of the king. . . . On the open road is his tent and he takes his food as necessity demands. . . . Many are his marches and vigils; his endurance of heat and cold, engagements with the foe, the worst and greatest of perils; often, perhaps, death itself — but a glorious death followed by rewards and a king's gifts. His life is toilsome in war; in peace it is joyous: The prize of valor, the crown [the wreath of victory] awarded . . . , to be called the king's friend, to stand at his side, to receive his salutation, to accept honors from the king's own hand, to be eminent among the king's people, and to play the mediator for his friends outside the Court in whatever they desire.

Come, then, soldier of Christ, with the aid of these ordinary parallels drawn from human considerations conceive the desire of everlasting goods. Set before yourself a life without house, homeland or possessions. Be free and at liberty from all worldly cares, lest desire of a wife or anxiety for a child fetter you. This cannot have place in the celestial warfare. . . . [2 Cor. 10:4]. Bodily nature does not exercise dominion over you. . . . Do not desire to leave behind you progeny upon earth . . . nor to cleave to fleshly unions, but to strive after spiritual ones—to exercise power over souls and to beget sons in the spirit. Follow the heavenly Bridegroom; withstand the assault of invisible foes; wage war against "principalities and powers" [Eph. 6:12], driving them out first from your own soul . . . and thereafter out of those who flee to you and, seeking . . . your counsel, cast themselves at your feet as their leader and champion. . . . Place your trust, most of all, in the arm of the great King, the mere sight of which makes His enemies fear and tremble. But whenever He wills that you too become holy through the endurance of perils and wishes to pit His forces against the Foe, then, . . . let your arms be invincible, your soul undaunted . . . and with ready will change your abode from land to land and from sea to sea. . . . Keep before your eyes Him who for our sake was afflicted . . . knowing that for the sake of Christ you also must be tested by affliction, and you will be victorious . . . for you follow a King who is a victor, and who wishes you to share in His victory.

But our discourse is not addressed to men only; for, members of the female sex are not rejected because of physical weakness but, chosen for the army of Christ by reason of their virility of spirit, they also battle on the side of Christ and fight no less valiantly than men. Some even win a greater renown. Of the number of these are they who compose the virgin throng. Of these are they who are pre-eminent in the combat for the confession of the faith and in the triumphs of martyrdom. Indeed, women as well as men followed after the Lord during His life on earth and both sexes ministered to our Savior.

Fight manfully, then, like good soldiers and run nobly your race for the everlasting crown [1 Cor. 9:24-5] [the athlete's wreath of trophy] in Christ Jesus, our Lord, to whom be glory for ever. Amen. (From Basil's *Introduction to the Ascetical Life, Ascetical Works,* trans. Sr. M. M. Wagner, *FC,* Vol. 9 [New York: Fathers of the Church, Inc., 1950], pp. 9-13; slightly alt.) For St. Basil and his concept of asceticism see pp. 109-11 above.

St. Benedict: Life in a Monastic Community

The Daily Services: 16. As the prophet says: "Seven times in the day do I praise You." This sacred number seven will thus be fulfilled by us if, at the hour of Lauds, Prime, Terce, Sext, None, Vespers, and Compline we perform the duties of our service. . . .

Greater Faults: 25. The brother who is held guilty of a graver fault shall be suspended from the [common] table and from the oratory [chapel]. None of the brothers may in any way keep him company. . . . He shall be alone at the labor enjoined upon him . . . "in order that his soul may be saved." [1 Cor. 5:5]

Spiritual Care: 27. The abbot shall show the utmost solicitude and care toward the brothers that offend. "Those who are well do not need a physician, but those who are sick" [Matth. 9:12]. And therefore he ought to use every means, as a wise physician, and dexterously send experienced elders to him, who, as it were secretly, shall console the wavering brother and lead him to humble himself and make amends. And they shall "comfort him lest he be overwhelmed by excess of grief" [2 Cor. 2:7] . . . and he shall be prayed for by all. For the abbot should know that he has undertaken the care of weak souls, not a tyranny over the strong.

Kitchen Duties: 35. The brothers shall wait on each other in turn; no one shall be excused from kitchen work unless he be kept from it by sickness or by preoccupation with some matter of great necessity. . . .

Reading at Meals: 38. At the mealtimes of the brothers there shall always be reading [by a common reader appointed for the week]. . . . And there shall be the greatest silence at table, so that no . . . voice except the reader's may be heard.

Of Daily Work: 48. Idleness is enemy of the soul. And therefore, at fixed times, the brothers ought to be occupied in manual labor, and, again, at fixed times, in sacred reading. . . . After the noon meal, moreover, they shall rest. . . . Let all things be done with moderation, on account of the fainthearted.

Reception of Guests: 53. All guests are to be received as Christ Himself, for He Himself said: "I was a stranger and you took me in" [Matth. 25:35]. And to all, fitting honor shall be shown. . . . A fast may be broken by the superior on account of a guest [to whom he shall keep company at meals]. . . . Chiefly in the reception of the poor and of pilgrims shall care most anxiously be shown; for in them Christ is received the more. . . .

Of Clothing: 55. Clothing shall be given to the brothers according to the nature of the place where they dwell, or the climate. . . . Concerning the color and size of all of which the monks shall not talk; but the clothing shall be such as can be found in the province where they are or as can be bought most cheaply. . . . And when new clothing is received, the brothers shall always right away return the old, to be kept in the wardrobe for the benefit of the poor. It is enough, moreover, for a monk to have two tunics and two cloaks. . . .

Election of an Abbot: 64. . . . The abbot . . . shall be well-versed in Scripture, so as to know how to bring forth from his treasure things new and old . . . he shall always put mercy over judgment [James 2:13] . . . and do nothing excessive. . . . He must be aware of his own frailty and remember that it is forbidden to break a bruised reed [Is. 42:3; Matth. 12:30]. We do not mean that he should permit the growth of vice, but that he use discretion and tenderness as he sees it expedient in the case of each one. . . .

He shall strive rather to be loved than feared. . . . He shall not be overmuch wedded to his own notion. . . . He shall use discernment and moderation, remembering the discretion of Jacob who said: "If I overdrive my flock they will die. . . ." [Gen. 33:13]. Discretion is the mother of all virtue. He must . . . so adjust his measures, that the strong may be led to press forward and the weak may not be disheartened. (From *The Rule of St. Benedict,* in Bettenson, pp. 165, 167, 170-1, 173, 176, 178-9, and *LCC,* Vol. XII, pp. 307, 311, 315-7, 321, 324-6, 332-3.) — On Benedict's *Rule* see pp. 112-14. Note that, while Benedict's *Rule* follows much of Basil's *Rule* (pp. 109 ff.), the brotherly dialog is not prominent here.

NO. 9 — AUGUSTINE

Confessions

1.1 "Thou art great, O Lord, and greatly to be praised" [Ps. 144:3]. "Thy power is great and of Thy wisdom there is no number" [Ps. 146:5]. To praise Thee is the wish of man who is but a part of Thy creation, man who carries about with him his own mortality, who carries about the evidence of his sin and the evidence "that Thou resistest the proud" [James 4:6; 1 Peter 5:5]. And yet, to praise Thee is the wish of man who is but a part of Thy creation. Thou dost bestir him so that he takes delight in praising Thee; for Thou hast made us for Thee and our heart is restless till it finds its rest in Thee.

1.3. . . . Dost Thou fill all the things which Thou fillest with Thy entirety? Or, because all things cannot encompass Thee in Thy entirety, do they contain part of Thee? And do all things contain the same part at once? Or does each contain its separate part, the bigger things bigger parts, the smaller things smaller parts? Is one part of Thee bigger, then, another smaller? Or art Thou everywhere entire and does no thing contain Thee wholly?

1.4. What art Thou, then, my God? What, I ask, but the Lord God? For, who is the Lord, but the Lord? Or who is God, besides our God? [Cf. Ps. 17:32]

O Highest, Best, most Powerful, most Omnipotent, most Merciful and most Just, most Hidden and most Evident, most Beautiful and most Strong, Stable and Incomprehensible, Immutable; moving all things, never new, never old, renewing all things [cf. Wisd. 7:27]; bringing the proud to senility and they know it not; ever active, ever quiet, gathering in and needing nothing, supporting and filling and protecting, creating and nourishing, perfecting, seeking, when nothing is lacking to Thee. Thou lovest, but art not disturbed by passion; Thou art "jealous," but free from care; Thou art angry, but calm; Thou changest Thy works, but not Thy plan.... What can anyone say — when he speaks of Thee? Yet, woe to those who do not speak of Thee; but, though they talk much, they say nothing.

1.5. Who will grant unto me to find repose in Thee? Who will grant unto me that Thou wilt come into my heart and inebriate it, so that I may forget my evils and embrace my one Good, Thee? What art Thou for me? Be merciful, that I may speak. What am I myself for Thee, that Thou dost command my love for Thee...? Hide not Thy face from me [Combining Ps. 142:7, Ex. 33:20, and Deut. 31:17]; let me die so that I may see it, lest I die.

1.6. Narrow is the household of my soul, for Thou to come into it: let it be enlarged by Thee. It lies in ruins: do Thou rebuild it. It has things within it which offend Thine eyes: I confess and know it. But who will cleanse it? Or to what other being than Thee shall I cry out: "from my secret sins cleanse me, O Lord, and from those of others spare Thy servant" [Ps. 18:13-14]?

1.30 . . . What was more filthy in Thy sight than I, [as a boy] when I even displeased such men [adults with questionable values] by telling countless lies to the servant in charge of me, to my teachers, and to my parents — moved by the love of games, fondness for the sight of frivolous shows, and by the disturbing process of imitating public spectacles. I also stole from my parents' cellar and table, either impelled by gluttony or in order to have something to give the boys who gave me in exchange the privilege of playing their game, in which they certainly took a pleasure equal to mine, yet nonetheless sold it. Even in this play, I frequently tried to win deceptive victories, because I was overcome by a vain desire for pre-eminence. What was I so unwilling to tolerate, and what did I argue about so fiercely, if I caught others doing it, except the same thing which I was doing to them? And if I myself was caught and shown to be guilty, I preferred to fight rather than to give way.

Is this the innocence of childhood? It is not, Lord; it is not . . . O my God. These are the very things which pass from pedagogues and teachers, from the nuts and balls and birds of childish sport, to governors and kings, to gold, estates, and slaves—these very things pass in sequence with the successive years of growth to maturity, just as greater penalties take the place of the teacher's rod.

2.4 . . . I wanted to steal, and I did it compelled by no want, unless it be by my lack of justice and disgust thereat and my plentitude of iniquity. For, I stole what I already possessed in abundance and of much better quality. Nor did I desire to enjoy the thing itself which was the object of my inclination to steal, but the very act of stealing, the sin itself.

There was a pear tree near our vineyard which was laden with fruit that was attractive neither in appearance nor in taste. In the dead of night—for we had prolonged our playing in the vacant lots, according to our usual unhealthy custom, until then—we crept up to it, a gang of youthful good-for-nothings, to shake it down and despoil it. We carried away huge loads, not as a treat for ourselves, but just to throw to the pigs. Of course, we did eat a few, but we did so only to be doing something which would be pleasant because forbidden.

Look at my heart, O God, look at my heart, which

Thou hast pitied in the depths of the abyss. Look at my heart; may it tell Thee now what it sought in this—that I might be evil without any compensation and that for my evil there might be no reason except evil. It was filthy and I loved it. I loved my own destruction. I loved my own fault; not the object to which I directed my faulty action, but my fault itself, was what I loved, my vile soul leaping down from Thy support into extinction, not shamefully coveting anything, but coveting shame itself. (St. Augustine, *Confessions*, trans. V. J. Bourke, in *FC*, Vol. 5 [New York: Fathers of the Church, Inc., 1953], pp. 3 f., 6 ff., 39-41.) — For Augustine's life and his *Confessions* see pp. 117 ff. and 125 ff.

Augustine on Grace

We for our part assert that the human will is so divinely aided toward the doing of righteousness that, besides being created with the free choice of his will and besides the teaching which instructs him how to live, he [man] receives also the Holy Spirit, through which there arises in his heart a delight in and a love of that supreme and unchangeable Good which is God: and this arises even now, while man still walks by faith and not by sight. That by this pledge, as it were, of the free gift [of God] he may burn to cleave to his Maker and be on fire to approach to a share in that true light; that from Him from whom he has his being he may also derive his blessedness. A man's free choice avails only to lead him to sin if the way of truth be hidden from him. And when it is plain to him what he should do and to what he should aspire, even then, unless he feel delight and love therein, he does not perform his duty, nor undertake it, nor attain to the good life. But so that we may feel this affection, "the love of God is shed abroad in our hearts" not through the free choice which springs from ourselves, but "through the Holy Spirit which has been given to us" [Rom. 4:5]. (From Augustine's anti-Pelagian treatise *On the Spirit and the Letter*, 5, trans. in Bettenson, p. 77, slightly alt.) — For the Pelagian controversy, see pp. 123 ff.

SUGGESTIONS FOR FURTHER READING

For more chronologically-oriented surveys several inexpensive books are available. The most popular treatment is in Roland Bainton's *Christendom*, Vol. 1 (New York: Harper & Row, 1964). Henry Chadwick, *The Early Church* (Baltimore, Md.: Penguin Books, 1967) covers the first six Christian centuries. W. H. C. Frend's *The Early Church* (New York: Lippincott, 1966), while not going beyond the mid-5th century, is very lively. J. G. Davies, *The Early Christian Church* (New York: Anchor paper, Doubleday, 1967), covering the same period, is a compromise between narrative history and a systematic treatment of recurring themes, such as worship, by periods. All of the latter three books contain extensive bibliographies. For an analysis of the development see the forthcoming book by Jaroslav Pelikan, *The Making of the Catholic Tradition*.

For the social and cultural history of the times see A. H. M. Jones, *The Latter Roman Empire 284-602* (New York: Oxford U. Pr., 1964), and his paperback of primary sources, *History of Rome Through the 5th Century* (New York: Harper & Row, 1970), vol. 2 being relevant for the Christian period. For maps and art see F. van der Meer and C. Mohrmann, *Atlas of the Early Christian World* (New York: Nelson, 1958). *The Horizon History of Christianity* by Roland Bainton (New York: American Heritage, 1964) has beautiful color reproductions. The best historical dictionary is F. L. Cross, ed., *Oxford Dictionary of the Christian Church* (New York: Oxford U. Pr., 1957 and 1966).

SUGGESTIONS FOR FURTHER READING

For the development of doctrine see J. N. D. Kelly's excellent *Early Christian Doctrines*, 2nd ed. (New York: Harper & Row, 1960); his *Early Christian Creeds* (New York: Longmans, 1952) is fascinating but more specialized. A comprehensive guide to the church fathers is Johannes Quasten, *Patrology*, Vols. 2 and 3 (Westminster, Md.: Newman Press, 1953 and 1961). For interesting sketches of these great men see Hans v. Campenhausen, *Fathers of the Greek Church* (New York: Pantheon Bks., Random House, 1959) and his *Men Who Shaped the Western Church* (New York: Harper, 1965). For the history of worship see Gregory Dix's classic, *The Shape of the Liturgy* (London: Dacre Press, 1945). Bernhard Poschmann, *Penance and the Anointing of the Sick* (New York: Herder & Herder, 1964) is a penetrating study of the penitential discipline. H. R. Niebuhr and D. D. Williams, *Ministry in Historical Perspectives* (New York: Harper, 1956) is valuable.

For the history of the papacy see B. J. Kidd, *The Roman Primacy to A.D. 461* (London & New York: Macmillan Co., 1936) and Pierre Batiffol's classical *Gregory the Great* (London: Burns, 1929). For the history of the monastic movement see Herbert B. Workman, *The Evolution of the Monastic Ideal* (Boston: Beacon Press, paper, 1962). For the monumental figure and contribution of Augustine see Peter R. L. Brown, *Augustine of Hippo* (Berkeley: U. of California Pr., 1967) and Roy W. Battenhouse, ed., *A Companion to the Study of St. Augustine* (New York: Oxford U. Pr., 1955). The paperbacks by Henri Marrou, *St. Augustine and His Influence* (New York: Harper, 1958) and Erich Przywara, *An Augustinian Synthesis* (New York: Harper, 1958) contain brief and arresting selections from Augustine's writings.

The interested reader is especially directed to the various series indicated in our Readings from Primary Sources and in the Notes. They contain extremely helpful introductions to and priceless documents of the ancient Christians themselves. All of the great church fathers can be found there.

INDEX

Abbot 102, 167
Advent 47-48
Africa 23, 25-26, 37, 91, 93, 117
Alaric 23
Alexandria 26, 60, 64, 68-69, 73, 78, 90, 93
Allegory 77-78
Ambrose 20, 28, 31, 36, 83, 88, 105, 118
Anointing 37, 42
Anthony, St. 101
Antioch of Syria 26, 33, 68-69, 73, 78, 90, 93
Apocrypha 76, 107
Apollinaris 68
Apostles' Creed 62
Archbishop 90
Arian 27, 60, 62-64
Arius 60-64, 148
Armenia 16, 38, 74
Art 15, 25, 49-52, 114
Ascension Day 46
Ascetic 100-101, 164
Ascetic radicals 102-8
Athanasius 56, 61, 64-65, 68, 109, 143-47
Augustine of Canterbury 27, 97
Augustine of Hippo 26, 38, 67, 88, 95, 105, 117-27, 168-71
  Confessions 117, 126, 168
Baptism 28, 34-39, 44, 55-57, 65, 133-35
Baradaeus, Jacob 74
Barbarian 20, 24, 38-39, 97-98
Basil the Great 65-66, 88, 109-14, 164
  Rules 110-12, 114
Basilica 52, 84, 86
Benedict of Nursia 112-15, 166
Benedictine Rule 113-15, 166-68
Bishop 17, 20, 24, 27, 30, 37, 64, 82-89, 132, 154
Byzantium 23, 25
Calendar 16, 43-48
Canon 27, 76-77
Canon laws 87, 141-43
Cappadocians 69, 109
Cassian 112, 114, 160
  Conferences 114, 162
Catacombs 50-51
Catechumen 16, 32-34, 44-45
Cathedral school 84
Catholic 66, 78
Celebration of redemptive events 46-47
Celtic monasticism 111-12
Chalcedonian 73-75
Christ
  person and natures of 67-75, 151-52
  revelation of God 58-60
Christianization 15-16
Christmas 16, 47-48
Christology 49, 56, 67-75, 148-53
  Christus Pantocrator 31, 52
  Christus victor 57
Chrysostom 26, 33, 36, 78, 87-88, 109
Church (building) 31, 49-50, 52
Church and society 15-23
Church-state relations 17-18, 25-26
Church year 29-30
City of God 26, 126
Clergy 82, 121-22
Collect 33, 138-39
Columba 27, 112
Confession of sins 32, 41-42, 103
Confessor 41, 103, 112
Confirmation 37
Constantine 13-15, 19, 23, 33, 36, 43, 62, 87, 89, 99, 130
Constantinople 23, 25, 64, 69, 90-91, 94
Contraception 119
Controversies 17, 60, 65-69, 71, 123, 131
Coptic Christians 74
Councils 27, 87, 90
  of Chalcedon 72-75
  of Constantinople 64-65, 68

SUGGESTIONS FOR FURTHER READING

For the development of doctrine see J. N. D. Kelly's excellent *Early Christian Doctrines*, 2nd ed. (New York: Harper & Row, 1960); his *Early Christian Creeds* (New York: Longmans, 1952) is fascinating but more specialized. A comprehensive guide to the church fathers is Johannes Quasten, *Patrology*, Vols. 2 and 3 (Westminster, Md.: Newman Press, 1953 and 1961). For interesting sketches of these great men see Hans v. Campenhausen, *Fathers of the Greek Church* (New York: Pantheon Bks., Random House, 1959) and his *Men Who Shaped the Western Church* (New York: Harper, 1965). For the history of worship see Gregory Dix's classic, *The Shape of the Liturgy* (London: Dacre Press, 1945). Bernhard Poschmann, *Penance and the Anointing of the Sick* (New York: Herder & Herder, 1964) is a penetrating study of the penitential discipline. H. R. Niebuhr and D. D. Williams, *Ministry in Historical Perspectives* (New York: Harper, 1956) is valuable.

For the history of the papacy see B. J. Kidd, *The Roman Primacy to A.D. 461* (London & New York: Macmillan Co., 1936) and Pierre Batiffol's classical *Gregory the Great* (London: Burns, 1929). For the history of the monastic movement see Herbert B. Workman, *The Evolution of the Monastic Ideal* (Boston: Beacon Press, paper, 1962). For the monumental figure and contribution of Augustine see Peter R. L. Brown, *Augustine of Hippo* (Berkeley: U. of California Pr., 1967) and Roy W. Battenhouse, ed., *A Companion to the Study of St. Augustine* (New York: Oxford U. Pr., 1955). The paperbacks by Henri Marrou, *St. Augustine and His Influence* (New York: Harper, 1958) and Erich Przywara, *An Augustinian Synthesis* (New York: Harper, 1958) contain brief and arresting selections from Augustine's writings.

The interested reader is especially directed to the various series indicated in our Readings from Primary Sources and in the Notes. They contain extremely helpful introductions to and priceless documents of the ancient Christians themselves. All of the great church fathers can be found there.

INDEX

Abbot 102, 167
Advent 47-48
Africa 23, 25-26, 37, 91, 93, 117
Alaric 23
Alexandria 26, 60, 64, 68-69, 73, 78, 90, 93
Allegory 77-78
Ambrose 20, 28, 31, 36, 83, 88, 105, 118
Anointing 37, 42
Anthony, St. 101
Antioch of Syria 26, 33, 68-69, 73, 78, 90, 93
Apocrypha 76, 107
Apollinaris 68
Apostles' Creed 62
Archbishop 90
Arian 27, 60, 62-64
Arius 60-64, 148
Armenia 16, 38, 74
Art 15, 25, 49-52, 114
Ascension Day 46
Ascetic 100-101, 164
Ascetic radicals 102-8
Athanasius 56, 61, 64-65, 68, 109, 143-47
Augustine of Canterbury 27, 97
Augustine of Hippo 26, 38, 67, 88, 95, 105, 117-27, 168-71
Confessions 117, 126, 168
Baptism 28, 34-39, 44, 55-57, 65, 133-35
Baradaeus, Jacob 74
Barbarian 20, 24, 38-39, 97-98
Basil the Great 65-66, 88, 109-14, 164
Rules 110-12, 114
Basilica 52, 84, 86
Benedict of Nursia 112-15, 166
Benedictine Rule 113-15, 166-68
Bishop 17, 20, 24, 27, 30, 37, 64, 82-89, 132, 154
Byzantium 23, 25
Calendar 16, 43-48
Canon 27, 76-77

Canon laws 87, 141-43
Cappadocians 69, 109
Cassian 112, 114, 160
Conferences 114, 162
Catacombs 50-51
Catechumen 16, 32-34, 44-45
Cathedral school 84
Catholic 66, 78
Celebration of redemptive events 46-47
Celtic monasticism 111-12
Chalcedonian 73-75
Christ
 person and natures of 67-75, 151-52
 revelation of God 58-60
Christianization 15-16
Christmas 16, 47-48
Christology 49, 56, 67-75, 148-53
Christus Pantocrator 31, 52
Christus victor 57
Chrysostom 26, 33, 36, 78, 87-88, 109
Church (building) 31, 49-50, 52
Church and society 15-23
Church-state relations 17-18, 25-26
Church year 29-30
City of God 26, 126
Clergy 82, 121-22
Collect 33, 138-39
Columba 27, 112
Confession of sins 32, 41-42, 103
Confessor 41, 103, 112
Confirmation 37
Constantine 13-15, 19, 23, 33, 36, 43, 62, 87, 89, 99, 130
Constantinople 23, 25, 64, 69, 90-91, 94
Contraception 119
Controversies 17, 60, 65-69, 71, 123, 131
Coptic Christians 74
Councils 27, 87, 90
 of Chalcedon 72-75
 of Constantinople 64-65, 68

INDEX

of Ephesus 49
of Nicaea 62-64
"Robber Council" 72
of Trent 76
Creed 27, 33, 56, 58, 60-65
Cross 31, 37-38, 58
Crucifix 57-58
Culture 15-16, 25
Cyprian 37, 55, 91, 154
Cyril 70-73
Damasus (pope) 106
Deacon 30, 32, 83, 86
Deaconesses 83, 86, 115
Dead, service in memory of 42
Death 57-58, 146
Decius 12
Deliverance 56
Desert Fathers 102-8, 159
Devotion 46, 48, 75
Diocletian 13, 101
Diogenes 104
Dioscorus 72
Discipline 39-42, 87, 140-43
Doctrine 55-78, 143-54
Donatists 120-22
Dura-Europos 49-50
East 24-26, 47, 61, 68, 74, 93
Easter 16-17, 36, 43-44
Ecumenical Council 62, 64, 68, 72
Egypt 74, 109, 113
Emperor 17, 19-20, 64, 72, 90-91, 132
England 16, 27, 97, 114, 158
Epiphany 47
Ethiopia 16, 74
Eucharist 28-34, 40-42, 56, 85, 135
Evagrius 114-15
Exorcism 34-35, 45, 83
Faith 55-58, 143-54
Fast days 45
Fathers 27
Flavian 20
Fortunatus, Venantius 31
Franks 112
Gaul 108-9, 111-13
Georgia 16, 38
Germany 112
Gloria in Excelsis 32
Gluttony 96

Gnostics 60, 105
God 17, 56-57, 59-66, 69-75, 148-49
Gothic invasion 10, 14, 23, 38
Greek-Orthodox 74
Gregorian chant 31
Gregory of Nazianzus 88, 109
Gregory of Nyssa 61, 68
Gregory the Great 10, 26, 31, 86, 88, 94-97, 105
Hades 58
Hermit 18, 41, 99-102
Holy Land 46
Holy Spirit 65-66, 153-54
Holy table (altar) 52
House-church 49
Humanitarian laws 19
Huns 24, 87
Hymns 31, 58, 139
Hypostases 66, 152
Ichthys 51
Icons 58
Incarnation 49, 56-57, 61, 143, 150
Incense 31
Infant baptism 37-38, 124
Inspiration 77
Instruction 34, 38, 42
Intercessor 48-49
Interpreting Scripture 77-78
Ireland 16, 27, 111-12
Jacobites 74
Jerome 105-8, 162-64
Jerusalem 46, 90, 135
Jews 15, 21, 43-44, 60
Justinian 15
Keys of the Kingdom 86, 92, 155
Kyrie eleison 32
Laity 82
Lapsed 12-13, 39, 140
Leadership 85-89, 95-96
Lent 44-45
Leo I (pope) 73, 94
Litany 32, 137-38
Liturgy 30-34, 37, 65, 135
Logos 59-61, 63, 68
Luther 95, 106, 111
Manicheanism 105, 117-20
Martin, St. 108
Martyrs 44, 46, 48, 50
Mary, Mother of God 48-49, 52, 70-75

Mass 32
Mesopotamia 104-5
Middle Ages 27, 32, 57-58, 82, 98, 115
Mission outreach 97-98, 114, 158
Monastery 109-16
Monasticism 99-116, 159-68
Monk 18, 24, 27, 41, 89, 99-116
Monophysite 72-75
Monte Cassino 113
Mosaics 52
Music 31
Muslims 75, 126
Nestorius 69-72, 151
Nicaea 62
Nicene Creed 60-65
Norms of doctrine 76-78
Nuns 99
Orders 83-84
Origen 16, 108
Pachomius 101-2, 109
Palestine 105, 107
Parish 84-85
Passion of our Lord 45
Passover 43-44
Pastoral Rule (Gregory) 95, 97, 158
Patrick, St. 27, 111, 139
Peasants 19
Pelagius 123-24
Penance 13, 35, 39-42, 45, 112, 140-43
Penitents 13, 33, 39-42, 45, 140-43
Pentecost 36, 44, 46
Persecution 10, 12-13, 35, 129
Persia 16, 74
Person of Christ 67-75
Persona 66
Petrine primacy 91-92
Philanthropy 14, 21, 86
Philo 60
Philosophy 104-5, 118-19
Physician of souls 94-97, 156
Pilgrimage 46
Poor 21, 86
Pope 26-27, 72, 82, 93-94
Prayer 29-31, 42, 56, 113
Predestination 125-26
Presbyter 30, 83-88
Priest 30, 83-85
Redemption 43-44, 46, 56-58, 143

Resurrection 57-58
Revelation 58-60, 145
Rome 23, 25-26, 46-47, 49, 86-87, 90, 92-94, 126-27
St. Maria Maggiore 49
Saints 34, 44, 48-49
Satan 58, 103
Schism 25, 69, 73-74, 120-22
Scotland 16, 27, 112
Scripture 55, 76-78, 106-7, 109, 114
See 84, 90
Simeon Stylites 103
Sin, preoccupation with 95, 103
Slavery 19, 22
Socrates 104
Soldier 22
Son of God 60-61, 63
Spirit 66
Stephen, bishop of Rome 91-92
Stoic influence 19
Substance 63, 66
Sunday 19, 28-29, 43, 131
Symbol of Union 72-73
Symbols 50-51
Syria 16, 49, 74, 104
Syrian Liturgy 37
Teaching 55-78, 143-54
Team Ministry 83-84
Tertullian 37, 68, 117
Thanksgiving 28, 32, 34
Theodosius I 15, 20, 64, 69
Theodosius II 71-72
Tradition 78
Tribal unity 16, 38-39
Trinity 66-67, 73, 119
Typology 77
Vandals 23, 87, 93, 117
Vestment 30
Vincent of Lerins 78
Virginity 108-9, 162
Vows 110
Vulgate 106-7
War 22
Wedding 42
Week 19
Weekday service 42
West 23-26, 47, 68, 73, 82, 107
Word of God 59, 61, 143-47
World 17, 23, 61-62, 99
Worship 28-52, 65, 76-77, 133